Time I Am -3

An Inch Of Time

Cannot Be Bought With

A mile of gold

By
Dr. Sahadeva dasa

B.com., FCA., AICWA., PhD
Chartered Accountant

Soul Science University Press

www.TimeIAm.com

Readers interested in the subject matter of this
book are invited to correspond with the publisher at:
SoulScienceUniversity@gmail.com +91 98490 95990
or visit DrDasa.com

First Edition: April 2014

Soul Science University Press expresses its gratitude to the
Bhaktivedanta Book Trust International (BBT), for the use of quotes by
His Divine Grace A.C.Bhaktivedanta Swami Prabhupada.

ISBN 978-93-82947-09-7

Published by:
Dr. Sahadeva dasa for Soul Science University Press

Printed by:
Rainbow Print Pack, Hyderabad

To order a copy write to purnabramhadasa@gmail.com
or buy online: Amazon.com, rlbdeshop.com

By The Same Author

Oil-Final Countdown To A Global Crisis And Its Solutions

End of Modern Civilization And Alternative Future

To Kill Cow Means To End Human Civilization

Cow And Humanity - Made For Each Other

Cows Are Cool - Love 'Em!

Let's Be Friends - A Curious, Calm Cow

Wondrous Glories of Vraja

We Feel Just Like You Do

Tsunami Of Diseases Headed Our Way - Know Your Food Before Time Runs Out

Cow Killing And Beef Export - The Master Plan To Turn India Into A Desert By 2050

Capitalism Communism And Cowism - A New Economics For The 21st Century

Noble Cow - Munching Grass, Looking Curious And Just Hanging Around

World - Through The Eyes Of Scriptures

To Save Time Is To Lengthen Life

Life Is Nothing But Time - Time Is Life, Life Is Time

Lost Time Is Never Found Again

Spare Us Some Carcasses - An Appeal From The Vultures

Cow Dung - A Down-To- Earth Solution To Global Warming And Climate Change

Cow Dung For Food Security And Survival of Human Race

(More information on availability on DrDasa.com)

Contents

Preface

Managing time is important but there is something even more important. That is, where you invest your time. There is no use of saving time when your time expenditure is in the wrong direction.

What comes first, the compass or the clock? Before one can truly manage time (the clock), it is important to know where you are going, what your priorities and goals are, in which direction you are headed (the compass). Where you are headed is more important than how fast you are going.

After you have set your priorities, then you can set out to find time for it. This is where time management comes into picture. There is time, hidden in the nooks and crevices of your day. If you have the will, you will find it.

A person learned 3 languages by reading vocabulary cards while peeing. Normally a person spends 10-15 minutes a day doing this duty. There is nothing much that can be done in the loo anyway.

Another person learned 2 new skills while waiting for his phone to be answered. Average time is close to 10 seconds before a call gets answered. Several minutes a day can be saved by keeping some information cards in the pocket which can be leafed through during this period.

While taking shower, you can listen to an audio book. One person read over 50 books in 3 years while waiting for websites to load in his computer. Of course this was way back when internet was slow. But still it is slow in many countries.

With the available technology, you can carry your office and library in your notebook computer or Ipad. A whole world has moved inside these electronic devices. Technology can be a great time waster or great time saver, it depends on you.

Dr. Sahadeva dasa
1st April 2014
Secunderabad, India

A Note On The Book Format

This book is based on One Victory A Day™ format. The chapters are arranged date wise. A reader need not read the book serially. He can open any chapter and he will find something useful for the day.

According to surveys, 80% of the books bought don't get read beyond 10% of their contents. They just sit in the shelves and this is especially true in recent times.

The thickness of the book acts as a deterrent, especially due to lack of time. Desperation grows and book lands in the shelf.

In One Victory A Day™ format, the book need not be completed. The idea is to read the chapter related to the day, and then understand, digest, assimilate and implement the information. That is improving life in small measures or changing life one day at a time. Throughout the day, you can try to reflect on and implement the newfound information.

Most of the books bought are not read fully because the reader can not relate the information to his or her life. Purpose of knowledge is not entertainment but betterment of life. Purpose of information is transformation, otherwise it's a waste of time. Ingestion of information without assimilation is like intake of food without digestion.

To scale a highrise, we go up one step at a time. To finish our meal, we eat one morsel at a time. A skyscraper is constructed one brick at a time. And an ocean is nothing but an assembly of many drops. This is the power of small. A big target, when broken down into small steps, becomes easily attainable.

People who are not into reading should cultivate the habit of reading in small installments. Phenomenal achievements can be accomplished by consistent and daily improvements. Good reading is as essential as clean air and water. Anything done regularly becomes a habit.

The mind's garden will produce whatever we sow in it. Daily we are being bombarded with a massive dose of undesirable information. The only way to counteract it is through assimilation of desirable information.

Nido Qubein's says, "One of the greatest resources people cannot mobilize themselves is that they try to accomplish great things. Most worthwhile achievements are the result of many little things done in a single direction."

Time

A Great Advice

Chanakya was an Indian philosopher and royal advisor. He authored the ancient Indian political treatise called Arthasastra. As such, he is considered to be one of the pioneers of the field of economics and political science in India, and his work is thought of as an important precursor to classical economics.

He is widely credited for having played an important role in the establishment of the Maurya Empire. As a mark of tribute, the area where all foreign embassies are located Delhi is called Chanakya puri.

He composed the following verse as an advise:

ayusah ksana eko 'pi na labhyah svarna-kotibhih
na cen nirarthakam nitih ka ca hanis tato 'dhika

Even a moment of one's lifetime could not be returned in exchange for millions of dollars. Therefore one should consider how much loss one suffers if he wastes even a moment of his life for nothing.   --Chanakya Pandita

Time is free, but it's priceless. You can't own it, but you can use it. You can't keep it, but you can spend it.
~ Harvey Mackay`

Time Management

2000 Years Ago

Chanakya's Time Management For Kings

In Chapter XIX, "The Duties of a King" in Book I, "Concerning Discipline" of the Arthasástra, Chanakya describes how to measure a day and what a king must do in each part of the day.

Time Measurement

"He shall divide both the day and the night into eight nálikas (1½ hours).

According to the length of the shadow (cast by the projecting piece on a sundial called gnomon):

The shadow of three purushás (36 angulás or inches),

Of one purushá (12 inches),

Of four angulás (4 inches),

And absence of shadow denoting midday are the four one-eighth divisions of the forenoon;

Like divisions (in the reverse order) in the afternoon."

Time Management (Day Time)

During the first one-eighth part of the day, he shall post watchmen and attend to the accounts of receipts and expenditure; (6 am to 7.30 am).

During the second part, he shall look to the affairs of both citizens and country people; (7.30 am to 10 am).

During the third, he shall not only bathe and dine, but also study; (10 am to 11.30am).

During the fourth, he shall not only receive revenue in gold (hiranya), but also attend to the appointments of superintendents; (11.30 am to 1 pm).

During the fifth, he shall correspond in writs (patra sampreshanena) with the assembly of his ministers, and receive the secret information gathered by his spies; (1 pm to 2.30 pm).

During the sixth, he may engage himself in his favourite amusements or in self-deliberation.

During the seventh, he shall superintend elephants, horses, chariots, and infantry.

During the eighth part, he shall consider various plans of military operations with his commander-in-chief. At the close of the day, he shall observe the evening prayer (sandhya vandanam).

Time Management (Night Time)

In ancient India, they had devices to keep track of time at night also. Chankya's advise for the night is as follows:

During the first one-eighth part of the night, he shall receive secret emissaries;

During the second, he shall attend to bathing and supper and study;

During the third, he shall enter the bed-chamber amid the sound of trumpets and enjoy sleep during the fourth and fifth parts;

Having been awakened by the sound of trumpets during the sixth part, he shall recall to his mind the injunctions of the scriptures as well as the day's duties;

During the seventh, he shall sit considering administrative measures and send out spies;

During the eighth division of the night, he shall receive benedictions from sacrificial priests, teachers, and the high priest, and having seen his physician, chief cook and astrologer, and having saluted both a cow with its calf and a bull by circumambulating round them, he shall get into his court.

Or in conformity to his capacity, he may alter the timetable and attend to his duties. When in the court, he shall never cause his petitioners to wait at the door, for when a king makes himself inaccessible to his people and entrusts his work to his immediate officers, he may be sure to engender confusion in business, and to cause thereby public disaffection, and himself a prey to his enemies.

He shall, therefore, personally attend to the business of gods, of heretics, of Bráhmans learned in the Vedas, of cattle, of sacred places, of minors, the aged, the afflicted, and the helpless, and of women;—all this in order (of enumeration) or according to the urgency or pressure of those works.

All urgent calls he shall hear at once, but never put off; for when postponed, they will prove too hard or impossible to accomplish. Having seated himself in the room where the sacred fire has been kept, he shall attend to the business of physicians and ascetics practising austerities; and that in company with his high priest and teacher and after preliminary salutation (to the petitioners).

Accompanied by persons proficient in the three sciences (trividya) but not alone lest the petitioners be offended, he shall look to the business of those who are practising austerities, as well as of those who are experts in witchcraft and Yóga.

Of a king, the religious vow is his readiness to action; satisfactory discharge of duties is his performance of sacrifice; equal attention to all is the offer of fees and ablution towards consecration.

In the happiness of his subjects lies his happiness; in their welfare his welfare; whatever pleases himself he shall not consider as good, but whatever pleases his subjects he shall consider as good.

Hence the king shall ever be active and discharge his duties; the root of wealth is activity, and of evil its reverse. In the absence of activity acquisitions present and to come will perish; by activity he can achieve both his desired ends and abundance of wealth.

Reference

Satya Sarada Kandula

V. K. Subramanian (1980). Maxims of Chanakya: Kautilya. Abhinav Publications. pp. 1–. ISBN 978-0-8364-0616-0.

S. K. Agarwal (1 September 2008). Towards Improving Governance. Academic Foundation. p. 17. ISBN 978-81-7188-666-1.

L. K. Jha, K. N. Jha (1998). "Chanakya: the pioneer economist of the world", International Journal of Social Economics 25 (2–4)

Subjective Time

And Your Control Over It

There are two types of time: clock time and real time. In clock time, there are 60 seconds in a minute, 60 minutes in an hour, 24 hours in a day and 365 days in a year. All time passes equally. When someone turns 50, they are exactly 50 years old, no more or no less.

In real time, all time is relative. Time flies or drags depending on what you're doing. Two hours at the train station can feel like 12 years. And yet our 12-year-old children seem to have grown up in only two hours.

Which time describes the world in which you really live, real time or clock time?

The reason time management gadgets and systems don't work is that these systems are designed to manage clock time. Clock time is irrelevant. You don't live in or even have access to clock time. You live in real time, a world in which all time flies when you are having fun or drags when you are doing your taxes.

The good news is that real time is mental. It exists between your ears. You create it. Anything you create, you can manage. It's time to remove any self-sabotage or self-limitation you have around "not having enough time," or today not being "the right time" to start a business or manage your current business properly.

There are only three ways to spend time: In thoughts, conversations and actions. In Sanskrit these are called manasa, vacha, karmana. Regardless of the type of business you own, your work will be composed of those three items.

Reference:
Joe Mathews, Don Debolt And Deb Percival

When The Time Takes Off

Consider for a moment the price of an airplane ticket. Each airplane has a limited amount of space. And the goal of the airline is to fill the airplane as much as possible.

When an airplane leaves the gate with empty seats, the price of those seats immediately drops to $0.00.

Once the plane lifts off, the opportunity to sell the empty seats is gone forever and the airline has absolutely no chance of getting a penny for it.

The value of an airline seat is directly related to whether it is occupied. Whether the price is $400.00 or $40.00, the seat has value only if there is a person sitting in it. After take-off, the chance for payment is history.

The same can be said about 'time'.

Each one of us has a specific amount of time that goes by with every moment.

Men talk of killing time, while time quietly kills them.
~Dion Boucicault

Lost or wasted time cannot be recovered. It is gone the moment that it passes.

Once a second is behind you, it cannot be replicated or returned.

The value of an unused minute drops to zero the moment it passes.

We Are Living

In Exponential Times

The world is changing more rapidly than ever before and that rate of change is accelerating.

One video about the rapid progression of information technology was shown at a Sony executive conference last year. Here are some excepts:

The first text message was sent in 1992. Today, the number of messages sent every day exceeds the number of people on Earth.

It took radio 38 years to reach 50 million people, TV 13 years, the Internet 4 years, the iPod 3 years, and Facebook 2 years.

The number of internet devices in 1984 was one thousand, in 1992 one million, in 2008 one billion.

4 exabytes (4 x 10^19) of unique information will be generated this year: more that the previous 5,000 years combined.

The amount of technical information is doubling every year.

The most in-demand jobs of 2010 did not exist in 2004.

Some of today's most innovative and significant market-leading companies did not exist 20 years ago: Amazon and eBay were founded in 1995, Google in 1998, Wikipedia in 2001, Skype &

iTunes in 2003, Facebook in 2004, YouTube in 2005, Twitter in 2006.

3 out of 8 couples married last in year in US met online.

Over one billion registered users of Facebook as of today. Average Facebook page is visited 30 times a day.

There are about 5,40,000 words in English language, about 5 times as many as during Shakespear's times.

More than 10000 new books are published daily. It is estimated that a week's worth of Newyork times contains more information then a person would likely to come across in a life time in 18th century.

It is estimated that 1.5 Exabytes or 15 quintillion bytes, (15,000,000,000,000,000,000) of unique new information will be generated worldwide this year. That's estimated to be more than previous 5000 years.

Seth Godin wrote the following ten years ago and it still applies today: "There has never been a worse time for business as usual. Business as usual is sure to fail, sure to disappoint, sure to numb our dreams. That's why there has never been a better time for the new. Your competitors are too afraid to spend money on new productivity tools. Your bankers have no idea where they can safely invest. Your potential employees are desperately looking for something exciting, something they feel passionate about, something they can genuinely engage in and engage with."

"Within our rapidly changing world, we might be apprehensive about the uncertainty and changes ahead. On the other hand, now is the best time to consider what these changes will cause and allow. Yes, there is now worldwide competition, but there are also worldwide marketplaces and opportunities. Opportunities can be found by challenging the status quo. Technology and innovation can be applied to solve a variety of problems in a variety of places.

In a worldwide marketplace, there is need for innovation and creativity in emerging and developed countries alike. Flexibility and adaptability are two of the most important traits required for success in our rapidly changing times. Those who succeed will be comfortable and confident in taking on new challenges."

Information Explosion

One aspect of exponential times is the information explosion. Information is exploding exponentially. For example, now there are thirty-one billion searches on Google every month. In 2006, it was 2.7 billion. That's a thirteen-fold increase in just three years.

To whom were these questions addressed before Google?

In order to keep up with this information explosion, engineers have been working at a breakneck pace to increase the efficiency and capacity of computers and other devices that process and store information. Every year, fifty quadrillion transistors are produced. That is more than six million for every human on the planet.(George Gilder, Wired, January 1998, p. 40)

Look at the exponential growth of Internet devices. In 1984, there were a thousand. By 1992, there were one million. By 2008, there were one billion and the number is about to exceed 15 billion.

Cisco IBSG Report

A 2011 Cisco IBSG report states:

"Looking to the future, Cisco IBSG predicts there will be 25 billion devices connected to the Internet by 2015 and 50 billion by 2020. It is important to note that these estimates do not take into account rapid advances in Internet or device technology; the numbers presented are based on what is known to be true today"

(2011 Cisco IBSG Report)

Intel: Rise of the Embedded Internet

Published 2009, an Intel report states,

"We are now on the threshold of a fourth phase in the evolution of the Internet. Intel calls this the Embedded Internet, a network space where billions of intelligent embedded devices will connect with larger computing systems, and to each other, without human intervention. In support of this concept, John Gantz of IDC forecasts 15 billion devices will be communicating over the network by the year 2015"

Ericsson Report

A report by Ericsson, published in February 2011, predicts more than 50 billion connected devices by next decade.

The vision of more than 50 billion connected devices will see profound changes in the way people, businesses and society interact. With ubiquitous mobile broadband-enabled internet access, connectivity and networking are becoming completely independent of location. Combined with falling prices for communication modules, connectivity services and embedded computing, the drivers for new services and functionality – broadband ubiquity, cost of connectivity, and openness and simplicity – will lead to more efficient business models and improved lifestyle for individuals and society. We are already heading full-speed towards connectivity for everyone. In 2010, more than twice as many connected devices as subscribers were added to carrier networks in the US market.

"Make a sandcastle with you? Of course, darling. What about Thursday 3.15pm?"

To understand how the number of connected devices could reach more than 50 billion over the next decade, it is worth considering

some high-level, macro-economic trends and statistics. As a few examples, by 2020 there will be:

3 billion subscribers with sufficient means to buy information on a 24-hour basis to enhance their lifestyles and improve personal security. In mature markets, these customers will typically possess between 5-10 connected devices each.

1.5 billion vehicles globally, not counting trams and railways.

3 billion utility meters (electricity, water and gas).

A cumulative 100 billion processors would be shipped, each capable of processing information and communicating.

Our Biggest Challenge

In fact, this may be our biggest challenge in the twenty-first century. There is so much information that most of us are having a difficult time trying to make sense of all the data. Facts, figures, and statistics are coming at us at an accelerating rate. That is why we need to evaluate everything we see, read, and hear in order to make sense of the world around us.

The cosmic situation is giving us all facility to reestablish this relationship with God and return to Godhead. This should be our mission in life. Everything we need is bring supplied by God -- land, grain, fruits, milk, shelter and clothing. We only have to live peacefully and cultivate Krsna consciousness. That should be our mission in life. We should therefore be satisfied with what God has supplied in the form of food, shelter, defense and sex, and should not want more and more and more. The best type of civilization is one that ascribes to the maxim of "plain living and high thinking." It is not possible to manufacture food or sex in a factory. These and whatever else we require are supplied by God. Our business is to take advantage of these things and become God conscious.

~ Srila Prabhupada (On The Way To Krishna : 5)

Technology

Has Overtaken Humanity

Albert Einstein had no idea of what's going on today, but even way back in 1940's he didn't like what he saw, "It has become appallingly obvious that our technology has exceeded our humanity."

What would have been his reaction to the present day scenario is any one's guess. The amount of new technical information is doubling every two years. That means for a student starting four year in a technical or college degree, half of what they learn in their first year of degree would be outdated by their third year. It is predicted to double every 72 hours by 2011.

3rd generation fibre optics, as per tests conducted by Alcatel, pushes 10 trillion bits of information per second through one strand of fibre. That's 1900 CDs or 150 million simultaneous phone calls every second. Current speeds are tripling every six months and it is expected to do so for next 20 years. Fibre is already there, they are just improving the switches on the ends. That mean the marginal cost effectively is zero.

Predictions are that epaper will be chaper than real paper.

47 million laptops were shipped worldwide in 2007.

Predictions are that by 2016, a super computer will be built that exceeds the "computational" capability of the human brain. By 2023, a $1000 computer will exceed the capabilities of human brain. Predictions are that by 2049, a $1000 computer will exceed the computational capabilities of human race.

People must be taught how to be satisfied with only what they need. In modern civilization there is no such education; everyone tries to possess more and more, and everyone is dissatisfied and unhappy. The Krishna consciousness movement is therefore establishing various farms, especially in America, to show how to be happy and content with minimum necessities of life and to save time for self-realization.

~ Srila Prabhupada (Srimad Bhagavatam 8.19.21)

An Overcommunicated World

We live in an overcommunicated world. Good etiquette insists we reply to all text messages within 10 minutes, be mindful of the mountain of emails building up in our inbox, and unfailingly return all 'missed calls' on our phones. Don't forget to regularly post something witty on Facebook, follow your best friends on twitter and utilise all the free airtime minutes on your contract! It is, after all, good to talk. But what is the net result of this web of exchange? Does it bring a greater sense of relationship and community? Is it a case of more connected, but further apart?

Silence, it's said, is the art of conversation. We often struggle with a quiet moment. When it does arise, most will instinctively grab their phone in a drastic attempt to engage their mind. To see someone sitting and doing absolutely nothing is rare! Even more unusual is to be with another person and not say anything. It feels awkward and uneasy. Yet silence is imperative – it forces us to understand, assimilate, reflect and think deeply about what is actually going on. Often times, however, in order to frantically fill those redundant moments we often end up generating substandard content to share with the world: meaningless, speculative and shoddy communication.

Don't get me wrong, there is definitely room for chitchat, niceties, and light-hearted exchange between humans. It would be unnatural to jump to the other extreme of strictly regulating our every word. The Bhagavad-gita, however, offers the over-arching model to guide speech. Words, Krishna recommends, should be truthful, pleasing and beneficial. How much of our written and verbal communication would make it through this filter? Along with freedom of speech, it may be worthwhile to remind people of their longstanding right to freedom of thought.

"Wise men speak because they have something to say; fools because they have to say something" (Plato)

Source:
By Sutapa Das, ISKCON News, Feb. 20, 2014

Prajalpa means talking nonsense. We assemble and go on talking for nothing, neither for this life, neither for that life. We should not talk... Suppose if we are gaining something materially, we may go on talking. Or if you are gaining some spiritually, we may talk. But if there is no gain, simply wasting time, that should not be done.
~ Srila Prabhupada (Bhagavad-gita 2.46-47 -- New York, March 28, 1966)

Record Breaking 64 Billion Messages

Sent Through Whatsapp In Just One Day

Whatsapp announced on April 2, 2014 that it had reached a new record for messages sent in a single day. And it's a whopping figure.

The popular messaging client for iOS and Android took to Twitter to break the news. Whatsapp stated that with 20 billion outgoing messages and 44 incoming messages handled in a single 24-hour period, the grand total came out to 64 billion.

Here's a little perspective on that number: Instagram recently announced that its users had posted 20 billion photos to the service. However, that was not a statistic for one day but the total number of photos shared in the history of the network.

That means that in one day, Whatsapp handled over three times as many requests as Instagram has since it launched three years ago.

That $19 billion acquisition by Facebook doesn't seem so extravagant now, does it?

Reference

Saqib Shah, 2 Apr 2014 in App News, Apps & Games

Another impediment is prajalpa, unnecessary talking. When we mix with a few friends, we immediately begin unnecessary talking, sounding just like croaking toads. If we must talk, we should talk about God consciousness.... people are interested in reading heaps of newspapers, magazines and novels, solving crossword puzzles and doing many other nonsensical things. In this fashion people simply waste their valuable time and energy. In the Western countries old men, retired from active life, play cards, fish, watch television and debate about useless socio-political schemes. All these and other frivolous activities are included in the prajalpa category.
~ *Srila Prabhupada (Nectar of Instruction: verse 2)*

Internet Addiction Disorder

Physical Damage To The Brain, Just Like Drugs

Internet addiction was first identified in the U.S. by Dr. Kimberly Young. In 1996, she presented the first paper on the topic at the American Psychological Association's annual conference held in Toronto entitled, "Internet Addiction: The Emergence of a New Disorder". Since then, studies have documented Internet Addiction in Australia, Italy, Pakistan, Iran, Germany, and the Czech Republic.

Researchers say that internet addiction can cause physical damage to the brain, just like drugs.

Internet addiction disrupts nerve wiring in the brains of teenagers, a study has found - causing a level of brain damage normally seen in 'heavy' substance abusers

Similar effects have been seen in the brains of people exposed to alcohol, cocaine and cannabis.

The discovery shows that being hooked on a behaviour can be just as physically damaging as addiction to drugs, scientists believe.

Brain scans show significant damage to white matter in the brain, proving, the researchers claim, that 'behavioural' addictions can cause physical brain damage in the same way as drug addictions.

Internet Addiction Disorder (IAD)

Internet addiction disorder (IAD) is a recently recognised condition characterised by out-of-control internet use.

Sufferers spend unhealthy amounts of time "online" to the extent that it impairs their quality of life.

Denied access to their computers, they may experience distress and withdrawal symptoms including tremors, obsessive thoughts, and involuntary typing movements of the fingers.

Until now research on IAD has focused on psychological assessments.

The new study, from China, used a Magnetic Resonance Imaging (MRI) technique to look at its effects on brain structure.

Scans were carried out on 17 internet-addicted adolescents and 16 non-addicted individuals, and the results compared.

In the IAD-diagnosed teenagers, the scientists found evidence of disruption to 'white matter' nerve fibres connecting vital parts of the brain involved in emotions, decision making, and self-control.

A measurement of water diffusion called 'fractional anisotropy' (FA) was used which provides a picture of the state of nerve fibres. Low FA was an indicator of poor nerve fibre structure.

The researchers, led by Dr Hao Lei from the Chinese Academy of Sciences in Wuhan, wrote in the online journal Public Library

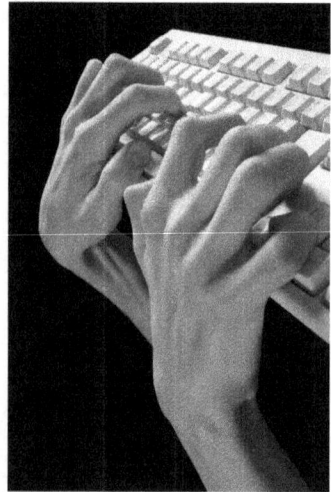

of Science ONE: 'Our findings suggest that IAD demonstrated widespread reductions of FA in major white matter pathways and such abnormal white matter structure may be linked to some behavioural impairments.'

'In addition, white matter integrity may serve as a potential new treatment target..'

Previous studies had shown abnormal white matter structure in the orbito-frontal regions of the brains of people exposed to alcohol, cocaine, cannabis, methamphetamine and ketamine, said the researchers.

They added: 'Our finding that IAD is associated with impaired white matter integrity in the orbito-frontal regions is consistent with these previous results.'

The scientists suspect the damage is caused by disrupted myelin, the fatty insulating sheath that coats nerve fibres and helps them to function.

Commenting on the findings, Dr Henrietta Bowden-Jones, consultant psychiatrist at Imperial College London, said: 'This type of research exploring the differences between normal brains and brains of people who suffer from internet addictions is groundbreaking as it makes clear neuroimaging links between internet addiction and other addictions such as alcohol, cocaine and cannabis amongst others.'

'We are finally been told what clinicians suspected for some time now, that white matter abnormalities in the orbito-frontal cortex and other truly significant brain areas are present not only in addictions where substances are involved but also in behavioural ones such as internet addiction.'

Currently, internet addiction is officially classified as an 'Impulse Control Disorder' (ICD) rather than a 'genuine' addiction. Further studies with larger numbers of subjects would be needed before

consideration could be given to reclassifying it, said Dr Bowden-Jones.

She added: 'I have seen people who stopped attending university lectures, failed their degrees or their marriages broke down because they were unable to emotionally connect with anything outside.'

In China, Korea, and Taiwan, internet addiction disorder is considered a serious epidemic now.

Reference:

Rob Waugh, 12 January 2012, The Dailymail, UK

---

labdhva sudurlabham idam bahu-sambhavante
manusyam arthadam anityam apiha dhirah
turnam yateta na pated anu mrtyu yavan
nihsreyasaya visayah khalu sarvatah syat
"This human form of life is obtained after many, many births, and although it is not permanent, it can offer the highest benefits. Therefore a sober and intelligent man should immediately try to fulfill his mission and attain the highest profit in life before another death occurs. He should avoid sense gratification, which is available in all circumstances."
~ Srimad Bhagavatam 11.9.29

Clinic For Internet Addicts

Many countries have opened clinics to treat internet addicts. In 2014, the first Internet Congress on Internet Addiction Disorders (IAD) was held in Milan. Korea is the leader in this field as it has established the first comprehensive, national prevention and re-education program for Screen Addictions. China and Japan utilize inpatient care with internet addiction fasting camps.

Australia developed the first inpatient adolescent treatment program for internet addiction. Italy has inpatient centers in Milan and Rome. France uses early education as a prevention for technology addictions. In the U.S., Internet Gaming Addiction is now listed in Section 3 of the DSM-5 (The Diagnostic and Statistical Manual of Mental Disorders, Fifth Edition).

In USA, the first such clinic named 'reStart' was opened outside Seattle 'where high-tech companies are as common as cattle are in

Texas.' It claimed to be America's first residential detox centre for internet addicts.

Opened in 2009, reSTART offers counseling and psychotherapy – and up to 45 days 'cold turkey' away from the web.

For a little over $14,000, up to six people at a time can spend 45 days sweating out their insatiable urge to be umbilically connected to cyberspace. Think cold turkey as experienced by heroin junkies, and you get the general idea.

Residents are given counselling and psychotherapy, as well as encouraged to bond as a group in activities such as household chores, walks in the grounds and exercising.

The centre, in five acres about 30 miles out of Seattle, is the brainchild of Hilarie Cash, a therapist who had been treating patients with presumed internet addiction but only on a day-by-day basis.

"Do you mind if dinner is late? I found some leftover tuna casserole on eBay!"

She recorded her first case in 1994, with a patient so glued to video games that he forfeited his marriage and two jobs.

Cash points out that though countries such as China, South Korea and Taiwan have places that cyber addicts can seek help, America has been slow to recognise the condition.

ReSTART offers anyone who suspects they are suffering from internet addiction the opportunity to test the hypothesis with a behavioural survey which, helpfully, can be completed via the internet. Question 12, for example, asks: "Are you experiencing chronic exhaustion due to lack of sleep, weight gain from lack of exercise, poor general health from poor nutrition, or other physical health problem due to excessive internet use or video gaming?"

Ben Alexander was one of the centre's first residents. He told Associated Press that he needed to break free from a cycle of playing the video game World of Warcraft, which used to absorb almost his every waking minute. Now 19, he started playing the game when he was a first-year student at Iowa University. "At first it was a couple of hours a day. By midway through the first semester, I was playing 16 or 17 hours a day," he said.

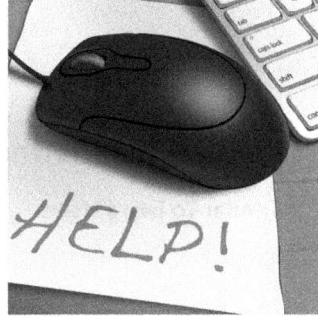

By comparison to the whizz-bang on the screen in front of him, the social life at university seemed extraordinarily dull. He came to see the game as an "easy way to socialise and meet people" – cyber though it was. Alexander eventually quit the university and sought help with his gaming.

References

Ed Pilkington , The Guardian, 4 September 2009

Dr. Young, The Center For Internet Addiction

> *sri-prahrada uvaca*
> *kaumara acaret prajno*
> *dharman bhagavatan iha*
> *durlabham manusam janma*
> *tad apy adhruvam arthadam*
>
> *Prahlada Maharaja said: One who is sufficiently intelligent should use the human form of body from the very beginning of life -- in other words, from the tender age of childhood -- to practice the activities of devotional service, giving up all other engagements. The human body is most rarely achieved, and although temporary like other bodies, it is meaningful because in human life one can perform devotional service. Even a slight amount of sincere devotional service can give one complete perfection.*
>
> *~ Srimad Bhagavatam (7.6.1)*

Web Addicts' Withdrawal Symptoms

Similar To Drug Users

Internet addicts can suffer a form of cold turkey when they stop using the web - just like people coming off drugs, according to a research reported by BBC.

A study by Swansea and Milan universities found young people had "negative moods" when they stopped surfing the net.

Heavy internet-users also tended to be more depressed, the research found.

Swansea University said around half of the 60 young people it studied spent so much time on the net that it had negative consequences for the rest of their lives.

When these people come off-line, they suffer increased negative mood - just like people coming off illegal drugs like ecstasy"

The results are part of a study looking at the negative psychological impacts of the internet.

The university said over the past decade internet addiction had became widely debated in medical literature.

Its research said the so-called addicts' web usage was varied, but it was common for them to gamble and access pornography online.

Prof Phil Reed, of Swansea University's college of human and health sciences, said: "Although we do not know exactly what internet addiction is, our results show that around half of the young people we studied spend so much time on the net that it has negative consequences for the rest of their lives.

"These initial results, and related studies of brain function, suggest that there are some nasty surprises lurking on the net for people's wellbeing.

"These results corroborate previous reports regarding the psychological characteristics and traits of internet users, but go beyond those findings to show the immediate effect of the Internet on the mood of those who are addicted."

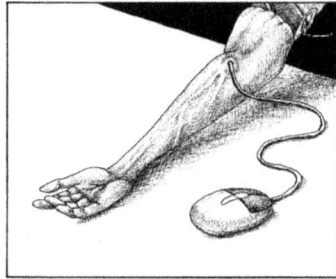

The study explored the immediate impact of internet exposure on the mood and psychological states of internet addicts and low internet-users.

The 60 volunteers, made up of 27 men and 33 women aged in their 20s, were given psychological tests to explore levels of addiction, mood, anxiety, depression and autism traits.

They were then given exposure to the internet for 15 minutes and re-tested for mood and anxiety.

The research found the mood of high internet-users suffered after internet use compared to low internet-users.

Scientists said this could possibly trigger them to log back on to the internet to "remove these unpleasant feelings".

Last year experts there said web addicts had brain changes similar to those hooked on drugs or alcohol.

They scanned the brains of 17 young web addicts and found disruption in the way their brains were wired up.

Reference

BBC, 19 June 2013

Internet Addiction

Missing Out On Life

D r. Kimberly Young has developed the Internet Addiction Diagnostic Questionnaire (IADQ). *Meeting five symptoms are necessary to be diagnosed.*

Signs of Internet Addiction

Do you feel preoccupied with the Internet (think about previous online activity or anticipate next online session)?

Do you feel the need to use the Internet with increasing amounts of time in order to achieve satisfaction?

Have you repeatedly made unsuccessful efforts to control, cut back, or stop Internet use?

Do you feel restless, moody, depressed, or irritable when attempting to cut down or stop Internet use?

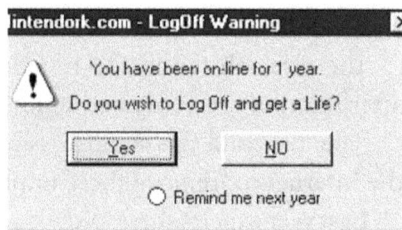

Do you stay online longer than originally intended?

Have you jeopardized or risked the loss of significant relationship, job, educational or career opportunity because of the Internet?

Have you lied to family members, therapist, or others to conceal the extent of involvement with the Internet?

Do you use the Internet as a way of escaping from problems or of relieving a dysphoric mood (e.g., feelings of helplessness, guilt, anxiety, depression)?

Other Symptoms Include:

Failed attempts to control behavior

Heightened sense of euphoria while involved in computer and Internet activities

Neglecting friends and family

Neglecting sleep to stay online

Being dishonest with others

Feeling guilty, ashamed, anxious, or depressed as a result of online behavior

Physical changes such as weight gain or loss, backaches, headaches, carpal tunnel syndrome

Withdrawing from other pleasurable activities

How To Avoid Internet Addiction

1. You can use a timer to keep track of time you spend online. Try to cut down the usage every week and in a few months bring it down to normal levels.

2. If a timer doesn't keep you on track, consider downloading parental control software-- some programs include time locks. Let someone else set the password to override so that you can get it in an emergency, but not at your whim. There is a Google Chrome browser extension called StayFocusd that can synchronize the list of blocked pages between multiple computers.

3. Delete accounts that you really don't need anymore. How many websites are there that you have accounts on that you don't 100% need? Twitter/Facebook is such a waste of time, and it's quite addicting. If you don't want to delete your account, just block the pages.

4. Delete your favorites (Keep important pages you might need for homework, etc.) -- YouTube videos, online friends' pages, all of it. If it's not essential for your work or for you to breathe, don't keep it.

5. Be sure to maintain lots of offline activities. Have plenty of things to do that you enjoy. If you don't have other hobbies, start looking for some. And volunteering can be a great way to get you out and about doing something useful/helpful.

6. Monitor your feelings when you're online and offline. Are you able to recognize when you've spent too long online? If not, you have a problem!

7. Know when to turn the computer off and take a walk. It is important to carve out patches of time to allow for understanding and processing the information you have consumed. This might mean disconnecting electronically on purpose. A scary thought to some, but yes, power down your computer and gadgets and go for a walk. If you feel you have lost your concentration and productivity, it may be due to the stress that you give yourself by staring at a monitor for too long.

8. Get a hobby or an interest that doesn't involve the internet, video games, TV, cell phones, smartphones, portable media players or computers. Get involved with church, music, dancing, singing or outdoor activities. Go to bed on time and get a good night's rest. Keep up with the local events in your community. There may be talks, book signings etc.

9. Complete your studies. If you are a student then do your homework and study. This is a great thing to do right away when you get home. Read books or research at the library instead of browsing Wikipedia for information.

10. Help with meals. Your parents will be happier that you're helping out with dinner or dishes instead of chatting online. Cook

or bake something one night for the family. Anything that gets you off the computer for a while will help and increase your confidence that you can stay off even longer.

11. While hanging out with friends, avoid places that have free internet access such as coffee shops.

12. If you have a laptop, make sure to put it somewhere that you can remember but not somewhere that you see every day. Try keeping the lid closed when you are not using it; when the computer is not looking at you, you are less likely to use it. If you have a desktop PC, try not to go near it or put something over it like a sheet.

13. Use an alarm clock or timer. Before using your computer decide on a time limit such as 30 minutes. Set the clock or timer and make sure that you get off the computer when the time is up. Alternatively create a shutdown timer shortcut on your desktop (google search "shutdown timer" for tutorials). This can be programmed to shutdown your computer after a predesignated time after it has been activated.

14. Don't eat meals at your computer! Eating at a separate place will help you to not go online.

15. Close your Internet browser – Eliminate Internet distractions by keeping your browser closed when you're not using it. If you

repeatedly check personal email, or go on social networking sites like Facebook or Twitter, then log out of your account. If you're forced to take those few extra seconds to log in each time, it may remind you that it's time to get up and do something else.

When we start looking on the Internet for one thing, it's easy to get lost for 20 minutes or more.

I LOVE My Computer Because My Friends Live In It

16. Use special software – There are some useful software applications such asFreedom and Anti-Social that help eliminate online distractions. You can specify which websites you want to block, and set a timer for how long you want the block to remain active. Using technology like this to block access for yourself can be a big help.

Reference:

Dr. Kimberly Young, The Center For Internet Addiction

Moreno MA, Jelenchick LA, Christakis DA (2013). Problematic internet use among older adolescents: A conceptual framework. Computers and Human Behavior. 29, 1879–1887.

Meerkerk, G.-J. et al. (2009). The Compulsive Internet Use Scale (CIUS). CyberPsychology & Behavior.

yatha hi purusasyeha
visnoh padopasarpanam
yad esa sarva-bhutanam
priya atmesvarah suhrt

The human form of life affords one a chance to return home, back to Godhead. Therefore every living entity, especially in the human form of life, must engage in devotional service to the lotus feet of Lord Visnu. This devotional service is natural because Lord Visnu, the Supreme Personality of Godhead, is the most beloved, the master of the soul, and the well-wisher of all other living beings.

~ Srimad Bhagavatam (7.6.2)

Television

A Dangerous Time Sucker

And A Weapon Of Mass Distraction

The proposition that television can be addictive is proving to be more than a glib metaphor. The most intensive scientific studies of people's viewing habits are finding that for the most frequent viewers, watching television has many of the marks of a dependency like alcoholism or other addictions.

For instance, compulsive viewers turn to television for solace when they feel distressed, rather than only watching favorite programs for pleasure. And though they get temporary emotional relief while watching, they end up feeling worse afterward.

Television addiction can be defined as excessive, continual viewing of television for extended periods of time. Physical as well as emotional and social problems may result from serious forms of television addiction. Treatment including psychotherapy and guided counseling by professionals can help break the cycle of addiction to TV.

This condition is studied in television studies and this compulsion can be extremely difficult to control in many cases. It has many parallels to other forms of behavioral addiction, such as addiction to drugs or gambling, which create an altered mental state in the subject. It can occur at any age.

Studies

Studies have shown that 65 to 70% of Americans believe television is addictive. There are many anecdotal reports of TV addiction, but there have been few empirical studies on the matter.

Research has yet to define parameters for "normal" vs. "problem" television viewing. Studies define these differently depending on the research.

One study found that self-described addicts watched an average of 56 hours a week; the A. C. Nielsen Company reports the average for adults is just above 30 hours a week.

Recent studies have found that 2 to 12 percent of viewers see themselves as addicted to television: they feel unhappy watching as much as they do, yet seem powerless to stop themselves.

Compulsive Television Viewing

The most commonly used scale to measure television addiction includes using television as a sedative, even though it does not bring satisfaction; lacking selectivity in viewing; feeling a loss of control while viewing; feeling angry with oneself for watching so much, not being able to quit watching and feeling miserable when kept from watching it.

"They turn on the TV when they feel sad, lonely, upset or worried, and they need to distract themselves from their troubles," says Robert McIlwraith, a psychologist at the University of Manitoba. Dr. McIlwraith reported his findings on television addiction at the annual meeting of the American Psychological Association in Boston last August.

Wasting Valuable Life

Portraits of those who admit to being television addicts are emerging from the research. For instance, a study of 491 men and women reported this year by Robin Smith Jacobvitz of the University of New Mexico offers these character sketches:

A 32-year-old police officer has three sets in his home. Although he is married with two children and has a full-time job, he manages to watch 71 hours of television a week. He says, "I rarely go out anymore."

A 33-year-old woman who has three children, is divorced and has no job reports watching television 69 hours a week. She says, "Television can easily become like a companion if you're not careful."

A housewife who is 50, with no children, watches 90 hours of television a week. She says, "I'm home almost every day and my TV is my way of enjoying my day."

Now they are producing millions of sets. Simple they are used for wasting time. They must sell. And people are induced to purchase. And as soon as they purchase, they simply see television. Idol worship. And learning vicious things. Some unnecessary picture is produced there. They like to see it. Two train are coming and they are smashed. (laughs) I have seen some television. People are learning how to smash, how to steal, how to harass people. Things are being shown like that. Not that "You are soul. You are spirit soul. If you degrade yourself, you then get this." You make that television, that how transmigration of the soul is taking place. They have manufactured the machine, so utilize for your propaganda. We have got to do so many things. We can utilize everything. So if they are not used for Krsna's purpose they'll be used for committing disaster in the world. Just like the atomic bomb. They are meant for creating disaster, that's all.
~ Srila Prabhupada (Room Conversation -- July 2, 1974, Melbourne)

References

By Daniel Goleman, October 16, 1990, New York Times

How Viewers Grow Addicted To Television.

McIlwraith, Robert. ""I', addicted to television": the personality, imagination, and TV watching patterns of self-identified TV addicts". www.bnet.com.

http://www.scientificamerican.com/article.cfm?id=television-addiction-is-n-2002-02

McIlwraith, Robert; Robin Jacobvitz; Robert Kubey; Alison Alexander (November 1991).

Escape Couch Potato Syndrome

Beat Your Television Addiction

Tired of wasting the equivalent of two months of your life every year glued to the tube? Spending more than an hour sitting in front of the television each evening? Like kicking any habit, half the battle of TV addiction is acknowledging the problem and making the commitment to change. Assuming you have the commitment, here are specific tips on getting the job done:

1. Throw out the remote control. It's amazing how much less television you'll watch if you have to get up every time you want to change channels or adjust the volume. Plus, it eliminates all those hours you spend channel surfing.

2. Give your extra TVs to charity. Allow your home one TV in a room dedicated to nothing but reading or TV watching. Donate the rest to a school or charitable organization in your community. You'll not only get the tax deduction and a feeling that you did good, but it will be that much harder to veg out in front of the tube!

3. Only turn on the TV to watch a particular show, if at all you have to. In other words, don't just turn it on and go surfing for something worthwhile. Hours are quickly wasted, switching from one show to the next, watching all and none at the same time.

4. Then, when you sit down to watch a particular show, set a timer or an alarm clock in another room for the length of the show. When it beeps, you'll have to get out of your chair to turn it off, a signal to also turn off the tube.

5. Rearrange the furniture. Design your family room so that the television becomes not the focal point of the room, but an afterthought that requires twisting around or rearranging the furniture to view.

6. Hide the television. Put it behind an cupboard, hang a blanket over it, or stick it inside a cabinet. Do whatever you can to ensure it fades into the background and can't be seen for what it is — a dangerous time sucker.

7. Eat meals, especially dinner, with the television OFF.

8. Set a rule that you can't watch TV if the sun is shining. Instead, you have to go for a walk, ride a bike, or get some other kind of healthy physical activity for at least an hour before you can turn on the tube. This rule also works great for your kids or grandkids.

9. Set a rule that you must read 30 pages of a book before you can turn on the TV. Depending on how fast you read, you may never watch TV again!

10. Create a list of one-hour evening projects. List everything you can possibly dream of: cleaning a particularly messy cupboard, organizing recipes, touching up the paint on your bedroom walls, sharpening kitchen knives, sorting through your sewing materials. Then create an old-fashioned job jar, and try to do one each evening.

12. Switch to outdoor activities. Get outdoors every night. Make it a point to leave your home or apartment at least once after dinner, if only for a short walk around the block.

16. Change your TV-viewing chairs. Make them somewhat hard and upright — chairs you don't want to lounge in for hours.

Move your most comfy chairs to the living room, and use them for listening to music and reading.

17. Say no any show in which you are watching a person talk. It is rare that a television interview or conversation is deeply insightful.

Reference:

Readers Digest

"Television Addiction: Theories and Data Behind the Ubiquitous Metaphor". American Behavioral Scientist (35 (2)): 104–121.

Horvath, Cary (September 2004). "Measuring Television Addiction". Journal of Broadcasting & Electronic Media 378: 378.

If there is no newspaper, they think life is horrible. But you won't find a piece of newspaper in our temple, because they have stopped talking all nonsense. Only this Bhagavad-gita, Bhagavata. This is called vacamsi vaikuntha-gunanuvarnane. They are no more interested with this nonsense talking of the newspaper. Vacamsi vaikuntha-gunanuvarnane. This is advancement of spiritual life. I have heard one story from a gentleman, how newspaper is important in Western country. We have seen also big, big bunch of newspaper thrown at every door. They subscribe. So one priest was preaching among the miners in Sheffield, where there are many coal mines, in England. So he was speaking that "You become devotee, followers of Jesus Christ," and in this way he's preaching Bible. So one of the miners, he never heard of Bible nor Jesus Christ. So he inquired, "What is his number?" That means he thought Christ may be one of the miners, and they have got specific number. So he said, "No, you are mistaking. Jesus Christ is the Lord. He is not one of you workers, no. He's the Lord. So if you don't appreciate him, don't worship him, then you will go to hell." Then another man asked, "What is hell?" And he described that "Hell is very dark. It is very moist," and so on. "There is no air there, no light, and..." So they are living always in the mine. There was no response, because they are habituated with this hellish life. (laughing) So the description of hell did not appeal. Then the priest was intelligent, said, "You know, there is no newspaper." Then they said, "Oh, horrible!" (laughter) "It is horrible."

~ Srila Prabhupada (Srimad-Bhagavatam 3.26.31 -- Bombay, January 8, 1975

How I Gained Two Extra Months Per Year

Diary of a Recovered TV Addict

And Reclaimed My Life

My girlfriend doesn't own a TV; a fact that puzzled me when we first met. What does she do for entertainment, I wondered. How does she get the news? Doesn't she get bored? How can she live without Seinfeld?

I didn't ask her those questions directly though, because I really didn't care. In fact, on a deeper level, I respected and envied her for that choice.

There was a time when I watched 5-6 hours of television every day. As evening approached after a long, hard day, I'd plant myself on the couch and vegetate till I fell asleep around midnight. Eight hours later, I'd wake up with the TV still on and me still feeling tired.

If you do the math, at that rate, it works out to around 2000 hours over the course of a year. That's about three months. THREE MONTHS. In front of a TV. Hypnotized. Tuned

in, but zoned out. Disconnected from the real world. Ahh yes, life was grand.

Actually, life wasn't grand. In truth, it was quite the opposite, and TV had become a full-blown addiction; an escape mechanism. Medication for the deeper wounds and issues I refused to deal with in my life. For me, TV filled the void of an otherwise empty life; a life barely lived by a soul knocked to his knees and struggling to get back up.

There's more to the story, of course, but that's for another time. For now, it's enough to say that – although my legs are still a bit wobbly – this soul is back on his feet and moving forward; due in large part to a commitment to gradually wean myself off television.

What To Do With Two Extra Months Each Year

I'm three months into the weaning process, and I still watch television. After all, the Red Sox are back in action, and I need my occasional Seinfeld fix. But I've drastically reduced my TV time. In fact, as I look over the past week, I probably spent 10 hours in front of the tube versus 35 hours at the height of my addiction.

Effectively, that means I've gained 25 hours each week, which works out to nearly two months over the course of a year. Yes, that's huge, but it's not the real victory here. The real victory lies in the activities and habits I've developed to more productively and purposefully invest that extra time. Here's a short list of some of those activities, habits and their benefits.

1. Early to Bed, Early to Rise

"It is well to be up before daybreak, for such habits contribute to health, wealth, and wisdom."

Aristotle

Nowadays, I'm usually asleep by 10pm, and I wake up around 4am. For me, there's something magical about rising that early. It gives me a head-start on the day, and morning tends to be my most creative time.

Plus, I just feel more on-purpose with a schedule like this. In short, it's good for the soul.

2. I Read More Books

As a web worker, I do a ton of online reading. Reading from a monitor gets tiresome though, so I'm starting to enjoy books again. I melt into a comfy chair or the couch and get lost in the book. I jot notes in the margins and highlight key passages. I make notes and outlines in a notebook and collect ideas for my own book that I'm researching.

3. I Write More

Although not apparent on this blog, I write nearly every day. One of my morning rituals is morning pages, a daily writing practice in which you simply produce three hand-written pages of stream-of-consciousness writing. Nearly every writing book on the market tells you the best way to improve your writing is simply to write more. The morning pages ritual allows me to write without having to worry about actually publishing what I write. As I continue to practice in this way, I feel my writing starting to improve and flow more freely.

4. My Life Feels More Purposeful and Meaningful

I'm sure this is implied in the previous items, but it needs to be stated directly. For whatever reason, there are times in our life when we feel lost at sea; out of control, floating directionless and forever buffeted by the pounding waves of life. Much of last year was like that for me, and I believe my TV addiction was part cause and part symptom.

Several months ago, a long-time coaching client recited a quote that went something like this: "most people are living shorter and dying longer." The words hit me like a bucket of ice water in the face, because that's close to how I was feeling at the time. When I chose to break my TV addiction, I made a clear, purposeful statement to myself and the universe that it's time to stop dying and start living again.

Life is meant to be lived. Bigger. Brighter. Bolder.

References

Michael Pollock, Opimal Living Archives

Illusioned by the material energy, people are so engrossed in subject matters for sense gratification that they have very little time to understand the question of self-understanding, even though it is a fact that without this self-understanding all activities result in ultimate defeat in the struggle for existence.

~ *Srila Prabhupada (Bhagavad-gita 2.29)*

Sleep

The Little Death

Studies show that that human beings need 6-7 hour of sleep per day. But if you are hell bent on wasting time, you can sleep for more time. If you sleep for three more hours everyday, you can waste 3 hours of your life per day. Now calculate it:

3 hours per day = 21 hours per week= 90 hours per month= 1095 hour per year (365x3). Suppose you are going to live for 100 years, you can waste 109500 hours of your life. That is exactly 12.5 years. Thus just by sleeping three

THIS MODERN LIFE:
WORK   HOME   PLAY   SLEEP

Although one has a maximum of one hundred years of life, by sleeping one loses fifty years. Eating, sleeping, sex life and fear are the four bodily necessities, but to utilize the full duration of life a person desiring to advance in spiritual consciousness must reduce these activities. That will give him an opportunity to fully use his lifetime.
~ Srila Prabhupada (Srimad Bhagavatam 7.6.6)

hours extra per day, you can waste 12.5 years of your life! You can improve your sleeping capacity and sleep for more time, just in case you want to waste more time.

See this guy? He's obviously new in church. He hasn't yet learned the fine art of sleeping with his eyes open.

There are only 24 hours in a day, so obviously you can waste 24 hours per day at your best. It is a sad thing that we can not waste our precious time in advance. But do not worry, try your best and waste maximum time you have got. One day, you will realize that you have wasted all your life.

World is going on under the influence of kala, time. So people should be enlightened that "Don't remain asleep." Uttisthata jagrata prapya varan nibodhata. "Now you are civilized human being. You can read and write. You can understand." So jagrata: "Now get up, be awakened. Study this Vedic literature, especially the essence of Vedic literature, Srimad-Bhagavatam."

~ Srila Prabhupada (Srimad-Bhagavatam 3.26.17)

Power Nap

Recharging Power of A Siesta

In Promoting Performance And Learning

Doctors used to think afternoon sleepiness was the result of a big lunch. "But we've found that in the early afternoon there's a dip in body temperature, which causes sleepiness," says Michael Smolensky, a professor of environmental physiology at the University of Texas School of Public Health at Houston. Just as a similar decrease encourages you to shut down at bedtime, this midday dip can make you crave a siesta. An ideal nap, he says, should last 15 to 20 minutes. More than 30 and you may end up with sleep inertia and feel even more groggy when you wake up. Richard Schwab, codirector of the University of Pennsylvania Penn Sleep Center, in Philadelphia, says that early afternoon is indeed when your circadian rhythms (the pattern of physical and mental changes we each repeat every 24 hours) are "more likely to want your body to sleep."

Others may prefer to take power naps regularly even if their schedules allow a full night's sleep. Mitsuo Hayashi, PhD and Tadao Hori, PhD have demonstrated that a nap improves mental performance even after a full night's sleep.

Benefits

Power naps of less than 30 minutes—even those as brief as 6 and 10 minutes—restore wakefulness and promote performance and learning. A University of Düsseldorf study found superior memory recall once a person had reached 6 minutes of sleep, suggesting that the onset of sleep may initiate active memory processes of consolidation which—once triggered—remains effective even if sleep is terminated.

A Flinders University study of individuals restricted to only five hours of sleep per night found a 10-minute nap was overall the most recuperative nap duration of various nap lengths they examined (lengths of 0 min, 5 min, 10 min, 20 min, and 30 minutes): the 5-minute nap produced few benefits in comparison with the no-nap control; the 10-minute nap produced immediate improvements in all outcome measures (including sleep

"He said he was taking a '*power nap*' - that was three hours ago."

latency, subjective sleepiness, fatigue, vigor, and cognitive performance), with some of these benefits maintained for as long as 155 minutes; the 20-minute nap was associated with improvements emerging 35 minutes after napping and lasting up to 125 minutes after napping; and the 30-minute nap produced a period of impaired alertness and performance immediately after napping, indicative of sleep inertia, followed by improvements lasting up to 155 minutes after the nap.

For several years, scientists have been investigating the benefits of napping, both the power nap and much longer sleep durations as long as 1–2 hours. Performance across a wide range of cognitive processes has been tested. Studies demonstrate that naps are as good as a night of sleep for some types of memory tasks.

A NASA study led by David F. Dinges, professor at the University of Pennsylvania School of Medicine, found that naps can improve certain memory functions. In that NASA study, volunteers spent several days living on one of 18 different sleep schedules, all in a laboratory setting. To measure the effectiveness of the naps, tests probing memory, alertness, response time, and other cognitive skills were used.

The National Institute of Mental Health funded a team of doctors, led by Alan Hobson, MD, Robert Stickgold, PhD,

and colleagues at Harvard University for a study which showed that a midday snooze reverses information overload. Reporting in Nature Neuroscience, Sara Mednick, PhD, Stickgold and colleagues also demonstrated that "burnout" irritation, frustration and poorer performance on a mental task can set in as a day of training wears on. This study also proved that, in some cases, napping could even boost performance to an individual's top levels. The NIMH team wrote "The bottom line is: we should stop feeling guilty about taking that 'power nap' at work."

> "Whenever you find time -- you must find time -- ... read all these books, or chant. But when you are hungry, take prasadam. When you are sleepy, take a snap [that is, a nap], not very much, just to refresh. And go on, either chanting on the beads, reading the books, or talking about Krsna. In this way always remain in Krsna consciousness. ..."
>
> Referring to a short afternoon rest, Prabhupada called it a "snap" rather than a nap.
>
> ~ Srila Prabhupada Nectar 3

Sara Mednick conducted a study experimenting on the effects of napping, caffeine, and a placebo. Her results showed that a 60-90 minute nap is more effective than caffeine in memory and cognition.

Cardiovascular Benefits

The Washington Post of February 13, 2007 reports at length on studies in Greece that indicate that those who nap have less risk of heart attack.

The siesta habit has recently been associated with a 37 percent reduction in coronary mortality, possibly due to reduced cardiovascular stress mediated by daytime sleep (Naska et al., 2007).

References

Maas, James B.; Wherry, Megan L. (1998). Miracle Sleep Cure: The Key to a Long Life of Peak Performance. London: Thorsons. ISBN 978-0-7225-3644-5.

Wikipedia

McEvoy, RD; Lack, LL (2006). "Medical staff working the night shift: Can naps help?". The Medical journal of Australia 185 (7): 349–50. PMID 17014398.

Dhand, Rajiv; Sohal, Harjyot (2007). "Good sleep, bad sleep! The role of daytime naps in healthy adults". Current Opinion in Internal Medicine 6: 91. doi:10.1097/01. mcp.0000245703.92311.d0.

Lahl, Olaf; Wispel, Christiane; Willigens, Bernadette; Pietrowsky, Reinhard (2008). "An ultra short episode of sleep is sufficient to promote declarative memory performance". Journal of Sleep Research 17 (1): 3–10. doi:10.1111/j.1365-2869.2008.00622.x. PMID 18275549.

Brooks, A; Lack, L (2006). "A brief afternoon nap following nocturnal sleep restriction: Which nap duration is most recuperative?". Sleep 29 (6): 831–40. PMID 16796222.

"NASA: Alertness Management: Strategic Naps in Operational Settings". 1995. 2012-04-16.

Mollicone, Daniel J.; Van Dongen, Hans P.A.; Dinges, David F. (2007). "Optimizing sleep/wake schedules in space: Sleep during chronic nocturnal sleep restriction with and without diurnal naps". Acta Astronautica 60 (4–7): 354. doi:10.1016/j.actaastro.2006.09.022.

"The National Institute of Mental Health Power Nap Study". 2002-07-01. 2002-07-01.

What We Love To Do

We Find Time To Do

In truth, people can generally make time for what they choose to do; it is not really the time but the will that is lacking.

Where there is a will, there is a way. People always make time to do the things they really want to do.

Next time you hear some one say, "I am sorry, but I was just too busy to do this work", know for certain that he is not interested in that work.

No one is too busy in this world, it's all about priorities.

However filled up my stomach may be, there is always room for some dessert.

However crowded the streets may be, there is always room for presidential cavalcade.

However busy my day may look like, there is always room for something I love.

Successful people achieve so much in a day while many of us lament about not having enough time to even take 30 minutes off and take care of the machine which keeps working non-stop for us, i.e., our body.

Again its all about priorities and what I love.

The Thing

I Value Most In My Life

A young man learns what's most important in life from the guy next door.

It had been some time since Jack had seen the old man. College, career, and life itself got in the way. In fact, Jack moved clear across the country in pursuit of his dreams. There, in the rush of his busy life, Jack had little time to think about the past and often no time to spend with his wife and son. He was working on his future and nothing could stop him.

Over the phone his mother told him, "Mr. Belser died last night. The funeral is Wednesday."

Memories flashed through his mind like an old newsreel as he sat quietly remembering his childhood days.

THE MOST IMPORTANT THINGS IN LIFE AREN'T THINGS

Anthony J. D'Angelo

"Jack, did you hear me?"

"Oh sorry, Mom. Yes, I heard you. It's been so long since I thought of him. I'm sorry, but I honestly thought he died years ago," Jack said.

"Well, he didn't forget you. Every time I saw him he'd ask how you were doing. He'd reminisce about the many days you spent over 'his side of the fence' as he put it," Mom told him.

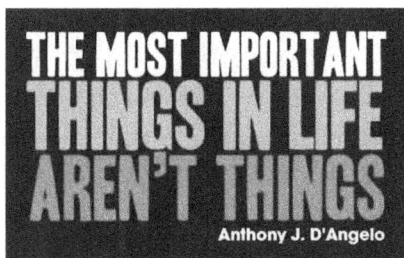

"I loved that old house he lived in." Jack said.

"You know, Jack, after your Father died, Mr. Belser stepped in to make sure you had a man's influence in your life," she said.

"He's the one who taught me carpentry," he said, "I wouldn't be in this business if it wasn't for him. He spent a lot of time teaching me things he thought were important. Mom, I'll be there for the funeral," Jack said.

As busy as he was, he kept his word. Jack caught the next flight to his hometown. Mr. Belser's funeral was small and uneventful. He had no children of his own and most of his relatives had passed away.

The night before he had to return home Jack and his Mom stopped by to see the old house next door one more time.

Standing in the doorway Jack paused for a moment. It was like crossing over into another dimension, a leap through space and time. The house was exactly as he remembered. Every step held memories. Every picture, every piece of furniture...Jack stopped suddenly.

"What's wrong, Jack?" his Mom asked.

"The box is gone," he said.

"What box?" Mom asked.

"There was a small gold box that he kept locked on top of his desk. I must have asked him a thousand times what was inside. All he'd ever tell me was, 'The thing I value most'," Jack said.

It was gone. Everything about the house was exactly how Jack remembered it except for the box. He figured someone from the Belser family had taken it.

"Now I'll never know what was so valuable to him," Jack said, "I better get some sleep. I have an early flight home, Mom."

It had been about two weeks since Mr. Belser died. Returning home from work one day Jack discovered a note in his mailbox. "Signature required on a package. No one at home. Please stop by the main post office within the next three days," the note read.

Early the next day Jack retrieved the package. The package was old and looked like it had been mailed a hundred years ago. The handwriting was difficult to read, but the return address caught his attention.

"Mr. Harold Belser" it read.

Jack took the package out to his car and ripped it open. There inside was the gold box and an envelope. Jack's hands shook as he read the note inside.

"Upon my death please forward this box and its contents to Jack Bennett. It's the thing I value most in my life". A small key was taped to the letter. His heart raced as tears filled his eyes. Jack carefully unlocked the box. There inside he found a beautiful gold pocket watch.

Running his fingers slowly over the finely etched casing, he unlatched the cover. Inside he found these words engraved:

"Jack, Thanks for your time! - Harold Belser."

"The thing he valued most...was...my time..and his time."

Reference

Story by Bob Perks © Bob Perks http://www.bobperks.com

Prajapati: ...Srila Prabhupada. You're very, very regulated, almost down to the minute in your activities. This is also a big help in utilizing time?

Prabhupada: Yes. Avyartha kalatvam. This should be our aim. Not a single moment is wasted. You should always remember. Not a single moment should be wasted. That is advised by Rupa Gosvami. Avyartha kalatvam. Vyartha means spoiling. Avyartha means not spoiling. One should be always conscious that "I am not wasting my time."

...on the street. The bums, they also utilize, they want to see that not a moment is wasted without drinking. (devotees chuckle) Yes, they actually do that. They want to drink only, twenty-four hours. As soon as the bottle is finished, they're finding somebody who will pay one dollar, and purchase another small bottle. They're doing this business only.

(Morning Walk -- January 5, 1974, Los Angeles)

4 Generations Of Time Management

The Evolution

C ovey argues that, as a field of management study, time management has gone through four stages:

1. Identifying tasks and recognizing demands on our time

2. Using calendars and appointment books to schedule and plan for the future

3. Planning ahead and prioritizing activities; applying personal values to the process of prioritization

4. Focusing on activities that are not urgent but are important

People who adhere to the fourth generation of time management focus on effectiveness and results, rather than efficiency and methods. They realize and prioritize the importance of relationships.

Covey recognizes that we often have different roles and needs within our lives, such as family, work, community, time for ourselves, and recreation or other activities. Covey's time management model is based on the assumption that we should manage time around what is important, not what is urgent, and that this should be carried out and planned across the different roles.

Stephen Covey pioneered this type of thinking several years ago but it is certainly worth repeating based on the incredible pressures we are all under in the area of time management. In a day when it is impossible to do everything that comes our way we must find ways to prioritize the important things and the discipline to say no to everything else.

The first wave or generation of time management could be characterized by simply taking notes and making checklists to try to keep track of all the things we needed to do. To some degree we still use this today but in a much more effective way.

The second generation started to use calendars and appointment books. The big improvement here was in planning ahead and making sure we had an idea of what we wanted to accomplish over a longer period of time. We all still use calendars today and they help us not only in planning but in daily execution as well.

The third generation brought into play the whole concept of prioritization into the process where we try on a daily, weekly, monthly or annual basis to identify those things that are most important and do them first and move the lesser items to the bottom of list. We started setting goals and incorporating those goals into our time planning which place a priority on efficiency.

The emerging fourth generation recognizes that time management is a misnomer because the ultimate challenge is not to manage time

maitreya uvāca
guna-vyatikarākāro
nirviśeso 'pratisthitah
purusas tad-upādānam
ātmānam līlayāsrjat
Maitreya said: Eternal time is the primeval source of the interactions of the three modes of material nature. It is unchangeable and limitless, and it works as the instrument of the Supreme Personality of Godhead for His pastimes in the material creation.
~ Srimad Bhagavatam 3.10.11

as much as it is to manage ourselves. This whole concept recognizes that just because we can do things faster today they might not be the right things to do.

The fourth generation mindset is that I will value relationships over results and I will always be open in the flow of my life to change direction on any given day when a greater priority comes into my life. The use of time is based on core values and is not driven by efficiency but effectiveness.

Reference
Dan Greer, Developing Leaders For Life.

Sharpen Your Axe

Improving efficiency is another way to save time. Time spent on improving efficiency or learning a new skill is always a good investment of one's time.

Once upon a time a very well-built woodcutter asked for a job with a timber merchant, and he got it.

The salary was really good and so were the work conditions. For that reason, the woodcutter was determined to do his best. His boss gave him an axe and showed him the area where he was supposed to work. The first day, the woodcutter brought 18 trees "Congratulations," the boss said. "Go on that way!"

Very motivated by the boss' words, the woodcutter tried harder the next day, but could bring 15 trees only.

The third day he tried even harder, but could bring 10 trees only.

Day after day he was bringing less and less trees. "I must be losing my strength", the woodcutter thought.

He went to the boss and apologized, saying that he could not understand what was going on.

"When was the last time you sharpened your axe?" the boss asked.

"Sharpen? I had no time to sharpen my axe. I have been very busy trying to cut trees..."

The care and attention you give yourself is an important investment of time. Scheduling time to relax, or do nothing, can help you rejuvenate both physically and mentally, enabling you to accomplish tasks more quickly and easily.

"HERE, YOU'RE ALLOWED TO SHARPEN YOUR CLAWS TO YOUR HEART'S CONTENT !"

The story is similar to that of a boatman who was so busy rowing he had no time to plug holes in his boat. Needless to say he drowned.

Many people are too busy to eat even. Hardly they find time to tuck in some snacks.

Good Time, Bad Time

Vs. The Right Time

Good and bad times are the two sides of the coin of life. Adversity is a fact of life. It can't be controlled. What we can control is how we react to it. The difference between stumbling blocks and stepping stones is how you use them.

G.I Jane says, "Pain is your friend; it is your ally. Pain reminds you to finish the job and get the hell home. Pain tells you when you have been seriously wounded. And you know what the best thing about pain is? It tells you you're not dead yet!"

"This time, like all times, is a very good one, if we but know what to do with it", Emerson says. The true test of a person character is how they stand during the test of adversity. Some one comments, "I learned there are troubles of more than one kind. Some come from ahead, others come from behind. But I've bought a big bat. I'm all ready, you see. Now my troubles are going to have trouble with me."

> *Make profit this side or that side. That is businessman. The businessman makes profit when the price is going down and when the price is going up. They make their profit. That is businessman.*
> *~ Srila Prabhupada (Morning Walk at Marine del Rey -- July 13, 1974, Los Angeles)*

One day a farmer's donkey fell in a well.

The animal cried piteously for hours as the farmer tried to figure out what to do. Finally he decided the animal was old, and the well needed to be covered up anyway; it just wasn't worth it to retrieve

the donkey. He invited his neighbors to come over and help him. They all grabbed a shovel and began to shovel dirt into the well.

When the donkey realized what was happening he cried out in panic. Then, to everyone's amazement, he quieted down. A few shovel loads later, the farmer finally looked down the well, and was astonished at what he saw. With every shovel of dirt that hit his back, the donkey was doing something amazing. He would shake it off and take a step up.

As the farmer's neighbors continued to shovel dirt on top of the animal, he would shake it off and take a step up. Pretty soon, everyone was amazed as the donkey stepped up over the edge of the well and trotted off!

Life is going to shovel dirt on you, all kinds of dirt. The trick to getting out of the well is to shake it off and take a step up. Each of our troubles is a stepping stone. We can get out of the deepest wells just by not stopping, never giving up! Shake it off and take a step up!

The Secret to Getting Done

More In Less Time

Are you overscheduling and underperforming? Adding some white space to your calendar can make you happier and more effective.

White Space is Breathing Space.

You most probably heard that work life balance is called the "holy grail of the 21st century." In bookstores, the bookshelves groan with books devoted to the topic, yet ironically enough, quite a few people just can't find the time to read them.

Graphic designers and layout people will tell you that white space is what makes it possible for us to register text on a printed page or a computer screen. White space gives order, context, and emphasis to what matters.

White space facilitates delight: it makes it possible for the contents of a page or of a life to be arranged in a pleasing way. It requites and allows artful choice. Without it, everything seems equally urgent, similarly important.

Because it is empty, it is tempting to fill white space when the pressure is on. If you've ever tried to read an email that isn't broken up into short paragraphs, you know what happens when too much content squeezes out the white space. It is hard to track meaning, hard to isolate key points, hard to know how to respond.

The same thing happens when there is not enough white space in our lives. When we steal time from the white space to make another meeting, start another project, make another call, we end up distracted, confused, and reactive. Depending on our individual styles, we may get irritable, weepy, bossy, or simply forgetful, none of which saves time, makes money, or engenders effective collaboration. In an ironic turnabout, we may start saying "no" to things we'd like to say "yes" to and vice versa. Play feels like work, work loses its charm, work life balance quits us.

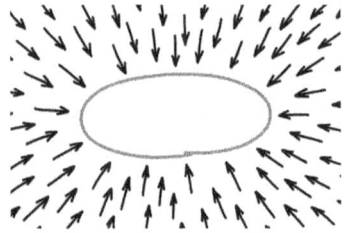

However, if we expand or maintain white space in times of great challenge, we will often notice that unexpected opportunities and solutions arise. When a problem is too big or complex to be solved with available resources, we have to go to another level to solve it. White space helps us find that other level and bring work life balance back, when pushing harder and moving faster won't work.

If there is not enough white space in your life to sustain work life balance, or if you need more white space than usual right now, take some time to revise your commitments and declare a moratorium on promises for a few days. If you are a manager, ask yourself how you can support your people in having the white space they need. It's not necessary to make a production of this; you can accomplish a good deal by simply keeping white space in mind as you assign tasks, evaluate performance, and manage the context and mood of your teams.

Caring for white space can allow the shape of what is truly important to emerge while giving us the breathing room to stay balanced and respond more completely and effectively, if at a slower pace.

If EVERYTHING Is Important, Then NOTHING Is Important

Let go of the feelings that you have to get it all done right now! This frenetic way of thinking is perpetuated in our society and it's very counterproductive. We all look very busy and important making calls, hurrying off to meetings, ticking off item after item that needs to be done to get through the day. Although your appointments, meetings and tasks are all very important, keep in mind the mantra that if EVERYTHING is important, then NOTHING is important!

More White Space Means Better Productivity

So, the next time your mind starts buzzing and you realize that you haven't had a second to stop and take a breath in your day... ask yourself... how much white space is in my day? Just like in advertising...the power is in the white space!

Reference

Molly Gordon, MCC Shaboom Inc. Life could be a dream, March 2008

Sara Caputo,, Business Productivity Coaching

Good Times

An Opportunity To Prepare For The Bad Times

Expect the best but be ready for the worst as well. It wasn't raining when Noah built the ark. It is often seen if something can go wrong, it will.

Material world is a precarious place. It's very nature is uncertainty and surprises. If some how sun is shining in your life, make hay and be prepared for the big freeze.

The Ant And Grasshopper

In a field one summer's day a grasshopper was hopping about, chirping and singing to its heart's content. An ant passed by, bearing along with great toil an ear of corn he was taking to the nest.

"Why are you working so hard?" he asked, "come into the sunshine and listen to my merry notes."

"But the ant went on her work. She said" I am lying in a store for the winter. Sunny days won't last for ever."

"Winter is so far away yet, "laughed the grasshopper back.

And when the winter came, the ant settled down in her snug house. She had plenty of food to last the whole winter. The grasshopper had nothing to eat so, he went to the ant and begged her for a little corn.

"No", replied the ant, "you laughed at me when I worked. You yourself sang through the summer. So you had better dance the winter away."

matra-sparsas tu kaunteya
sitosna-sukha-duhkha-dah
agamapayino 'nityas
tams titiksasva bharata

O son of Kunti, the nonpermanent appearance of happiness and distress, and their disappearance in due course, are like the appearance and disappearance of winter and summer seasons. They arise from sense perception, O scion of Bharata, and one must learn to tolerate them without being disturbed.

~ Bhagavad-gita, 2.14

Don't Do

Delegate

Delegation means assigning responsibility for a task to someone else, freeing up some of your time for tasks that require your expertise. Delegation begins by identifying tasks that others can do and then selecting the appropriate person(s) to do them. You need to select someone with the appropriate skills, experience, interest, and authority needed to accomplish the task. Be as specific as possible in defining the task and your expectations, but allow the person some freedom to personalize the task.

Occasionally check to determine how well the person is progressing and to provide any assistance, being careful not to take over the responsibility. Finally, don't forget to reward the person for a job well done or make suggestions for improvements if needed.

Another way to get help is to "buy" time by obtaining goods or service that save you a time investment. For example, paying someone to mow your lawn or clean your house, using a computerized system, or joining a carpool to transport your children to their extracurricular activities can allow you free time to devote to other activities.

Necessity of Delegation

If you work on your own, there's only a limited amount that you can do, however hard you work. You can only work so many hours in a day. There are only so many tasks you can complete in these hours. There are only so many people you can help by doing these tasks. And, because the number of people you can help is limited, your success is limited.

However, if you're good at your job, people will want much more than this from you.

This can lead to a real sense of pressure and work overload: you can't do everything that everyone wants, and this can leave you stressed, unhappy, and feeling that you're letting people down.

Those who delegate successfully, build a team of strong and successful people.

Why People Don't Delegate

To figure out how to delegate properly, it's important to understand why people avoid it. Quite simply, people don't delegate because it takes a lot of up-front effort.

After all, which is easier: designing and writing content for a brochure that promotes a new service you helped spearhead, or having other members of your team do it?

You know the content inside and out. You can spew benefit statements in your sleep. It would be relatively straightforward for you to sit down and write it. It would even be fun! The question is, "Would it be a good use of your time?"

"I start my day by making a list of everything I need to do . . . and who I can get to do it for me."

While on the surface it's easier to do it yourself than explain the strategy behind the brochure to someone else, there are two key reasons that mean that it's probably better to delegate the task to someone else:

- First, if you have the ability to spearhead a new campaign, the chances are that your skills are better used further developing the strategy, and perhaps coming up with other new ideas. By doing the work yourself, you're failing to make best use of your time.
- Second, by meaningfully involving other people in the project, you develop those people's skills and abilities. This means that next time a similar project comes along, you can delegate the task with a high degree of confidence that it will be done well, with much less involvement from you.

Delegation allows you to make the best use of your time and skills, and it helps other people in the team grow and develop to reach their full potential in the organization.

When To Delegate

Delegation is a win-win when done appropriately, however, that does not mean that you can delegate just anything. To determine when delegation is most appropriate there are five key questions you need to ask yourself:

"In the interest of overcoming my reluctance to delegate, starting Monday I want you to do all of my worrying for me."

- Is there someone else who has (or can be given) the necessary information or expertise to complete the task? Essentially is this a task that someone else can do, or is it critical that you do it yourself?
- Does the task provide an opportunity to grow and develop another person's skills?
- Is this a task that will recur, in a similar form, in the future?
- Do you have enough time to delegate the job effectively? Time must be available for adequate training, for questions

and answers, for opportunities to check progress, and for rework if that is necessary.

- Is this a task that I should delegate? Tasks critical for long-term success (for example, recruiting the right people for your team) genuinely do need your attention.

If you can answer "yes" to at least some of the above questions, then it could well be worth delegating this job.

Once you decide to delegate a job, use a Delegation Worksheet to keep record of the tasks you choose to delegate and who you want to delegate them to.

To Whom Should You Delegate?

The factors to consider here include:

1. The experience, knowledge and skills of the individual as they apply to the delegated task.

- What knowledge, skills and attitude does the person already have?
- Do you have time and resources to provide any training needed?

2. The individual's preferred work style.

- How independent is the person?
- What does he or she want from his or her job?

Once on a visit to Boston, Srila Prabhupada had a meeting with his ISKCON Press workers. Satsvarupa dasa complained to Prabhupada that he had so many duties in the temple that he was distracted in trying to do all of them and at the same time also do press work. Prabhupada said, "Real management means to delegate it to others."

~ Srila Prabhupada Nectar 2

- What are his or her long-term goals and interest, and how do these align with the work proposed?
3. The current workload of this person.
- Does the person have time to take on more work?
- Will you delegating this task require reshuffling of other responsibilities and workloads?

How Should You Delegate?

Use the following principles to delegate successfully:
1. Clearly articulate the desired outcome. Begin with the end in mind and specify the desired results.
2. Clearly identify constraints and boundaries. Where are the lines of authority, responsibility and accountability? Should the person:
- Wait to be told what to do?
- Ask what to do?
- Recommend what should be done, and then act?
- Act, and then report results immediately?
- Initiate action, and then report periodically?
3. Where possible, include people in the delegation process. Empower them to decide what tasks are to be delegated to them and when.
4. Match the amount of responsibility with the amount of authority. Understand that you can delegate some responsibility, however you can't delegate away ultimate accountability. The buck stops with you!
5. Delegate to the lowest possible organizational level. The people who are closest to the work are best suited for the task, because they have the most intimate knowledge of

the detail of everyday work. This also increases workplace efficiency, and helps to develop people.

6. Provide adequate support, and be available to answer questions. Ensure the project's success through ongoing communication and monitoring as well as provision of resources and credit.

7. Focus on results. Concern yourself with what is accomplished, rather than detailing how the work should be done: Your way is not necessarily the only or even the best way! Allow the person to control his or her own methods and processes. This facilitates success and trust.

8. Avoid "upward delegation." If there is a problem, don't allow the person to shift responsibility for the task back to you: ask for recommended solutions; and don't simply provide an answer.

9. Build motivation and commitment. Discuss how success will impact financial rewards, future opportunities, informal recognition, and other desirable consequences. Provide recognition where deserved.

10. Establish and maintain control.

- Discuss timelines and deadlines.
- Agree on a schedule of checkpoints at which you'll review project progress.
- Make adjustments as necessary.
- Take time to review all submitted work.

In thoroughly considering these key points prior to and during the delegation process you will find that you delegate more successfully.

Keeping Control

Now, once you have worked through the above steps, make sure you brief your team member appropriately. Take time to explain why they were chosen for the job, what's expected from them during the project, the goals you have for the project, all timelines and deadlines and the resources on which they can draw. And agree a schedule for checking-in with progress updates.

Therefore the king, Rsabhadeva, is advising, instructing His sons... He was retiring. Why He was retiring? He could enjoy His kingdom. Just like at the present moment, either a king or a family man does not retire. Even a poor man living in with family with great difficulties, but if you ask him to retire, he'll not be agreeable. We have asked many old men. He's suffering, he's not happy within his family members, but if I say, "Why you are taking so much trouble with the family? Why not come and live with us in Krsna consciousness society?" he'll not agree. Because he has no Vedic training. Up to the end of this life he'll stick to the family life. Many, many politicians... In our country we have seen many old politicians, seventy-five years old, eighty years old. Not only in our country, in other countries also. In your country, Great Britain, Mr. Churchill, unless he was forced to death, he would not give up politics. Our Gandhi, he was killed by another political group. Then he was forced to retire. When Gandhi attained independence, I requested him in a letter, "Mahatma Gandhi, now you started your struggle with the Britishers, that they should go and Indians should have their independence. Now you have attained independence and Britishers have gone. Now you preach Bhagavad-gita. You have got some influence. You are known throughout the whole world a very great saintly person, and you also pose yourself that you are a great scholar of Bhagavad-gita. Why don't you take up Bhagavad-gita and preach?" There was no reply. And he was still meddling with politics, so much so that his own assistants became disgusted. And it is said that he was planned to be killed. Just see how much intoxication of this materialistic way of life. He was considered a mahatma, a great personality, and he got his svarajya. The Britishers left India. Still, he would not give up politics. Still, he would stick -- unless he was forced to give up, he was killed. Similarly, Jawaharlal Nehru also. Nobody would retire voluntarily -- unless he is killed by somebody or he is killed by the laws of material nature. This is the disease. He cannot give it up. Daivi hy esa gunamayi mama maya duratyaya [Bg. 7.14]. The maya is so strong that even an old man advertising to be very pious man, he

Continued on the next page.......

Lastly, make sure that the team member knows that you want to know if any problems occur, and that you are available for any questions or guidance needed as the work progresses.

We all know that as managers, we shouldn't micromanage. However, this doesn't mean we must abdicate control altogether: In delegating effectively, we have to find the sometimes-difficult balance between giving enough space for people to use their abilities to best effect, while still monitoring and supporting closely enough to ensure that the job is done correctly and effectively.

........Continued from the previous page

cannot give up politics. Because maya is so strong, he's thinking, "If I leave political field, my countrymen will suffer, and so many disaster will happen." He's thinking like that.

But actually, things will go on. Many politicians came and gone. In your country there were many, many great politicians; they came and gone. But your country people are still living and they are going on. In Germany also, many Hitlers came and gone. Similarly, in India also many Gandhis came and gone. But things are going on. This is explained in the Bhagavad-gita:

prakrteh kriyamanani

gunaih karmani sarvasah

ahankara-vimudhatma

kartaham iti manyate

[Bg. 3.27]

Everything is being done by the laws of nature. You cannot change it. There is a plan, God's plan. It will go on. You don't have to bother yourself, that without you, everything will be topsy-turvied. No.

~ Srila Prabhupada (Lecture, Srimad-Bhagavatam 5.5.1 -- Tittenhurst, London, September 12, 1969)

Avoid Micromanagement

Let Others Use Their Brain And Free up Your Time

In business management, micromanagement is a management style whereby a manager closely observes or controls the work of subordinates or employees. Micromanagement generally has a negative connotation.

Merriam-Webster's Online Dictionary defines micromanagement as "management especially with excessive control or attention on details" In micromanagement, the manager not only tells a subordinate what to do but dictates that the job be done a certain way regardless of whether that way is the most effective or efficient one.

Symptoms

Rather than giving general instructions on smaller tasks and then devoting time to supervising larger concerns, the micromanager monitors and assesses every step of a business process and avoids delegation of decisions. Micromanagers are usually irritated when a subordinate makes decisions without consulting them, even if the decisions are within the subordinate's level of authority.

Micromanagement also frequently involves requests for unnecessary and overly detailed reports ("reportomania"). A micromanager tends to require constant and detailed performance feedback and to focus excessively on procedural trivia (often in detail greater than they can actually process) rather than on overall performance, quality and results. This focus on "low-level" trivia often delays decisions, clouds overall goals and objectives, restricts the flow of information between employees, and guides the various aspects of a project in different and often opposed directions. Many micromanagers accept such inefficiencies as less important than their retention of control or of the appearance of control.

It is common for micromanagers, especially those who exhibit narcissistic tendencies and/or micromanage deliberately and for strategic reasons, to delegate work to subordinates and then micromanage those subordinates' performance, enabling the micromanagers in question to both take credit for positive results and shift the blame for negative results to their subordinates.

"I would like you to be more self-reliant, show more initiative, and take greater personal responsibility — but check with me first!"

The most extreme cases of micromanagement constitute a management pathology closely related to, e.g., workplace bullying and narcissistic behavior. Micromanagement resembles addiction in that although most micromanagers are behaviorally dependent on control over others, both as a lifestyle and as a means of maintaining that lifestyle, many of them fail to recognize and acknowledge their dependence even when everyone around them observes it.

Effects

Because a pattern of micromanagement suggests to employees that a manager does not trust their work or judgment, it is a major factor in triggering employee disengagement, often to the point of promoting a dysfunctional and hostile work environment in which one or more managers, or even management generally, are labeled "control freaks." Disengaged employees invest time, but not effort or creativity, in the work in which they are assigned. A disempowered employee is an ineffective one – one who requires a lot of time and energy from his supervisor.

Severe forms of micromanagement can completely eliminate trust, stifle opportunities for learning and development of interpersonal skills, and even provoke anti-social behavior. Micromanagers of this severity often rely on inducing fear in the employees to achieve more control and can severely affect self-esteem of employees as well as their mental and physical health.

> **70% of employees feel they have worked for a micromanager**

Finally, the detrimental effects of micromanagement can extend beyond the "four walls" of a company, especially when the behavior becomes severe enough to force out skilled employees valuable to competitors.

Escaping Micromanagement

What can you do if you know you're exhibiting such behaviors – or are being subjected to them by a supervisor?

From the micromanager's perspective, the best way to build healthier relationships with employees may be the most direct: Talk to them.

It might take several conversations to convince them that you're serious about change. Getting frank feedback from employees is the hard part. Once you've done that, as executive coach Marshall Goldsmith recommends, it's time to apologize and change. This means giving your employees the leeway – and encouragement – to succeed. Focus first on the ones with the most potential, and learn to delegate effectively to them.

Part of being a good manager, one often lost on those of the micro variety, is listening. Managers fail to listen when they forget their employees have important insights – and people who don't

feel listened to become disengaged.

But there's a certain amount that you can do to improve the situation:

Help your boss to delegate to you more effectively by prompting him to give you all the information you will need up front, and to set interim review points along the way.

Volunteer to take on work or projects that you're confident you'll be good at. This will start to increase his confidence in you – and his delegation skills.

Make sure that you communicate progress to your boss regularly, to discourage him from seeking information just because he hasn't had any for a while.

Concentrate on helping your boss to change one micromanagement habit at a time.

References

Chambers, Harry (2004). My Way or the Highway. Berrett Koehler Publishers, San Francisco. 20 June 2008.

Wikipedia

Small Business Resource Centre (2006). Micromanagement. December 2009.

"Micromanage", via Merriam-Webster's Online Dictionary.

Dictionary.com (2008). Definition of micromanage.

Encarta Dictionary (2008). Definition of micromanage.

McConnell, Charles (2006). Micromanagement is Mismanagement. National Federation of Independent Business. Thomas, D. Narcissism: Behind the Mask (2010)

Bielaszka-DuVernay, Christina (2008). Micromanage at Your Peril. Harvard Business School Publishing Corporation.

Activity Logs

Finding More Time in Your Day

An Activity Log (also known as an Activity Diary or a Job Activity Log) is a written record of how you spend your time.

By keeping an Activity Log for a few days, you can build up an accurate picture of what you do during the day, and how you invest your time. You'll find that memory is quite a poor guide, and that keeping the Log is an eye-opening experience!

Your Activity Log will also help you understand whether or not you're doing your most important work during the right time of day. For instance, if you're more energetic and creative in the morning, you'd be better off doing your most important work during this time. You can then focus on lower energy tasks, such as responding to emails or returning calls, in the afternoon.

"Mr. McCoy has been expecting you. If you'll have a seat, he should be with you within the next 6 hours."

Activity Logs are also useful for helping you identify non-core activities that don't help you meet important objectives. For example, you might spend far more time than you think surfing the Internet, or getting coffee each afternoon. When you see how much time you're wasting on such activities, you can then change the way that you work to eliminate them.

How to Keep an Activity Log

To keep an Activity Log, open up a new spreadsheet and set up the following column headers:
* Date/Time.
* Activity description.
* How I feel.
* Duration.
* Value (high, medium, low, none).

Then, without changing your behavior any more than you have to, note down everything that you do, as you do it.

Every time you change activities, whether replying to email, working on a report or gossiping with colleagues, note down what the activity is, the time of the change, and how you feel (alert, flat, tired, energetic, and so on).

Then, at a convenient time, go back through your Activity Log and write down the duration of each activity, and whether it was a high, medium, low, or no value task. (Evaluate this based on how far it contributed to achieving your job goals.)

Learning from Your Activity Log

Once you've logged your time for a few days, analyze your Activity Log. You may be alarmed to see how much time you spend doing low value jobs!

You may also see that you are energetic in some parts of the day, and flat in other parts. A lot of this can depend on how you are, the rest breaks you take, when and what you eat, and the work that you're doing.

Once you've analyzed your Activity Log, you should be able to boost your productivity by applying one of the following actions to various activities:

1. Eliminate or delegate jobs that aren't part of your role, or that don't help you meet your objectives. These may include tasks that someone else in the organization should be doing (possibly at a lower pay rate) or personal activities such as sending non-work e-mails or surfing the Internet.

2. Schedule your most challenging tasks for the times of day when your energy levels are highest. That way, your work will be of better quality, and it should take you less time to do.

3. Minimize the number of times you switch between types of task. For example, could you check and reply to e-mails at only a few times of the day, or process all of your invoices at the same time each week?

4. Reduce the amount of time you spend on legitimate personal activities such as making drinks. (Take turns in your team to do this – it saves time and strengthens team spirit!)

Sometimes, spending too much time on low-value or low-priority tasks can be a symptom of procrastination.

Reference

Dianna Podmoroff, Mindtools.

Forster, Mark (2006-07-20). Do It Tomorrow and Other Secrets of Time Management. Hodder & Stoughton Religious. p. 224. ISBN 0-340-90912-9.

Procrastination

Procrastination is the practice of carrying out less urgent tasks in preference to more urgent ones, or doing more pleasurable things in place of less pleasurable ones, and thus putting off impending tasks to a later time, sometimes to the "last minute".

The pleasure principle may be responsible for procrastination; one may prefer to avoid negative emotions, and to delay stressful tasks. The belief that one works best under pressure provides an additional incentive to postponement of tasks.

Some psychologists cite such behavior as a mechanism for coping with the anxiety associated with starting or completing any task or decision. Other psychologists indicate that anxiety is just as likely to get people to start working early as late and the focus should be impulsiveness.

Schraw, Wadkins, and Olafson have proposed three criteria for a behavior to be classified as procrastination: it must be counterproductive, needless, and delaying. Similarly, Steel (2007) reviews all previous attempts to define procrastination, indicating it is "to voluntarily delay an intended course of action despite expecting to be worse off for the delay.". Sabini & Silver argue that postponement and irrationality are the two key features of procrastination; putting a task off is not procrastination, they argue, if there are rational reasons for doing so.

Procrastination may result in stress, a sense of guilt and crisis, severe loss of personal productivity, as well as social disapproval for not meeting responsibilities or commitments. These feelings combined may promote further procrastination.

While it is regarded as normal for people to procrastinate to some degree, it becomes a problem when it impedes normal functioning.

Chronic procrastination may be a sign of an underlying psychological disorder. Such procrastinators may have difficulty seeking support due to social stigma and the belief that task-aversion is caused by laziness, low willpower or low ambition. On the other hand many regard procrastination as a useful way of identifying what is important to us personally as it is rare to procrastinate when one truly values the task at hand.

Prevalence

In one of the earlier studies of academic procrastination, 46% of subjects reported that they "always" or "nearly always" procrastinate on writing a paper, whilst approximately 30% procrastinate on studying for exams or on reading for weekly assignments.

For a range of tasks, a quarter of subjects reliably reported that procrastination was a problem for them. Approximately 60%, however, indicated that they would like to reduce their procrastination.

Correlates

As noted above, procrastination is consistently found to be strongly correlated with conscientiousness, and moderately so with neuroticism.

Though the reasons for the relationship are not clear, there also exists a relationship between procrastination and 'eveningness'; that is to say that those who procrastinate more are more likely to go to sleep later and wake later. It is known that Conscientiousness increases across the lifespan, as does Morningness. Procrastination too decreases with age. However, even controlling for age, there still exists a relationship between procrastination and eveningness, which is yet to be explained.

Testing the hypothesis that procrastinators have less of a focus on the future due to a greater focus on more immediate concerns, college undergraduates completed several self-report questionnaires, which did indeed find that procrastinators focus less on the future.

I'm very busy doing things I don't need to do in order to avoid doing anything I'm actually supposed to be doing.

Researchers had also expected to find that procrastination would be associated with a hedonistic and "devil-may-care" perspective on the present; against their expectations, they found that procrastination was better predicted by a fatalistic and hopeless attitude towards life. This finding fits well with previous research relating procrastination and depression.

Justification

Individual coping responses to procrastination are often emotional or avoidant oriented rather than task or problem-solving oriented.

Avoidance: Where we avoid the locale or situation where the task takes place (e.g., a graduate student avoiding going to University).

Distraction: Where we engage or immerse ourselves in other behaviors or actions to prevent awareness of the task (e.g., intensive videogame playing or Internet surfing)

Trivialization: We reframe the intended but procrastinated task as being not that important (e.g., "I'm putting off going to the dentist, but you know what? Teeth aren't that important.").

Downward Counterfactuals: We compare our situation with those even worse (e.g., "Yes, I procrastinated and got a B- in the course, but I didn't fail like one other student did."). Upward counterfactual is considering what would have happened if we didn't procrastinate.

Humour: Making a joke of one's procrastination, that the slapstick or slipshod quality of one's aspirational goal striving is funny.

External attributions: That the cause of procrastination is due to external forces beyond our control (e.g., "I'm procrastinating because the assignment isn't fair").

Reframing: Pretending that getting an early start on a project is harmful to one's performance and leaving the work to the last moment will produce better results (e.g., "I'm most creative at 4:00 AM in the morning without sleep.").

levels of procrastination

1. non-procrastinator — does work early
2. Sunday-night slacker — slack all weekend
3. super slacker — 2-month projects, essays, labs etc. all in 1 night
4. master procrastinator — still procrastinating after deadline

Denial: Pretending that procrastinatory behaviour is not actually procrastinating, but a task which is more important than the avoided one.

Laziness: Procrastinating simply because one is too lazy to do their desired task.

Valorisation: Pointing out in satisfaction what we achieved in the meantime while we should have been doing something else.

Task or problem-solving oriented coping is rarer for the procrastinator because it is more effective in reducing procrastination. If pursued, it is less likely the procrastinator would remain a procrastinator. It requires actively changing one's behavior or situation to prevent a reoccurrence of procrastination.

References

Pychyl, T. (February 20, 2012). Due Tomorrow. Do Tomorrow. Psychology Today, http://www.psychologytoday.com/blog/dont-delay/201202/due-tomorrow-do-tomorrow Wikipedia

Fiore, Neil A (2006). The Now Habit: A Strategic Program for Overcoming Procrastination and Enjoying Guilt- Free Play. New York: Penguin Group. p. 5. ISBN 978-1-58542-552-5.

Steel, Piers (2010). The Procrastination Equation: How to Stop Putting Things Off and Start Getting Stuff Done. New York: HarperCollins. ISBN 978-0-06-170361-4.

Schraw, Gregory; Wadkins, Theresa; Olafson, Lori (2007). "Doing the things we do: A grounded theory of academic procrastination". Journal of Educational Psychology 99: 12. doi:10.1037/0022-0663.99.1.12.

Steel, Piers (2007). "The nature of procrastination: A meta-analytic and theoretical review of quintessential self-regulatory failure". Psychological Bulletin 133 (1): 65–94. doi:10.1037/0033-2909.133.1.65. PMID 17201571.

Pavlina, Steve. "How to Fall in Love with Procrastination".

Solomon, L. J., & Rothblum, E. D. (1984) Academic Procrastination: Frequency and Cognitive-Behavioural Correlates

Lee, Dong-gwi; Kelly, Kevin R.; Edwards, Jodie K. (2006). "A closer look at the relationships among trait procrastination, neuroticism, and conscientiousness". Personality and Individual Differences 40: 27. doi:10.1016/j.paid.2005.05.010.

Sabini, J. & Silver, M. (1982) Moralities of everyday life, p.128

Steel, P., Brothen, T., Wambach, C., (2001) Procrastination and personality, performance and mood [1]

Evans, James R. (8 August 2007). Handbook of Neurofeedback: Dynamics and Clinical Applications. Psychology Press. p. 293. ISBN 978-0-7890-3360-4.

Strub, RL (1989). "Frontal lobe syndrome in a patient with bilateral globus pallidus lesions". Archives of neurology 46 (9): 1024–7. doi:10.1001/archneur.1989.00520450096027. PMID 2775008.

Why Do We Procrastinate

Psychologists continue to debate the causes of procrastination. Drawing on clinical work, there appears to be a connection with issues of anxiety, low sense of self-worth, and a self-defeating mentality.

On the other hand, drawing on meta-analytical correlational work, anxiety and perfectionism have no – or at best an extremely weak – connection with procrastination. Instead, procrastination is strongly connected with lack of self-confidence (e.g., low self-efficacy, or learned helplessness) or disliking the task (e.g., boredom and apathy).

PROCRASTINATE
NOW
AND
PANIC
LATER

The strongest connection to procrastination, however, is impulsiveness.

Sabini and Silver argue that irrationality is an inherent feature of procrastination. That is to say that "putting things off even until the last moment isn't procrastination if there is reason to believe that they will take only that moment". As Steel et al. (2001) later explain, "actions must be postponed and this postponement must represent poor, inadequate, or inefficient planning".

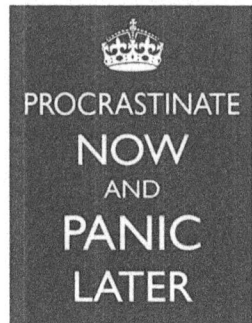

Based on integrating several core theories of motivation as well as meta-analytic research on procrastination is the temporal motivation theory. It summarizes key predictors of procrastination (i.e., expectancy, value and impulsiveness) into a mathematical equation.

Physiological Reasons

Research on the physiological roots of procrastination mostly surrounds the role of the prefrontal cortex. Consistent with the notion that procrastination is strongly related to impulsiveness, this area of the brain is responsible for executive brain functions such as planning, impulse control, and attention, and acts as a filter by decreasing distracting stimuli from other brain regions. Damage or low activation in this area can reduce an individual's ability to filter out distracting stimuli, ultimately resulting in poorer organization,

ayuktah prakrtah stabdhah
satho naiskrtiko 'lasah
visadi dirgha-sutri ca
karta tamasa ucyate

The worker who is always engaged in work against the injunctions of the scripture, who is materialistic, obstinate, cheating and expert in insulting others, and who is lazy, always morose and procrastinating is said to be a worker in the mode of ignorance.

In the scriptural injunctions we find what sort of work should be performed and what sort of work should not be performed. Those who do not care for those injunctions engage in work not to be done, and such persons are generally materialistic. They work according to the modes of nature, not according to the injunctions of the scripture. Such workers are not very gentle, and generally they are always cunning and expert in insulting others. They are very lazy; even though they have some duty, they do not do it properly, and they put it aside to be done later on. Therefore they appear to be morose. They procrastinate; anything which can be done in an hour they drag on for years. Such workers are situated in the mode of ignorance.
~Bhagavad gita (18.28)

a loss of attention and increased procrastination. This is similar to the prefrontal lobe's role in attention-deficit hyperactivity disorder, where underactivation is common.

Health Reasons

For some people, procrastination can be persistent and tremendously disruptive to everyday life. For these individuals, procrastination may be symptomatic of a psychological disorder.

Procrastination has been linked to a number of negative associations, such as depression, irrational behaviour, low self-esteem, anxiety, poor study habits, and neurological disorders such as ADHD. Others have found relationships with guilt and stress.

Therefore, it is important for people whose procrastination has become chronic and is perceived to be debilitating, to seek out a trained therapist or psychiatrist to see if an underlying mental health issue may be present.

In agreement with existing literature, Fritzsche et al. (2008) found that procrastination was related to general anxiety, specific anxiety about writing a paper, and with lower grades. They found that feedback from supervisors can play a crucial role in averting procrastination; "low procrastinators wrote their papers early, regardless of whether they received feedback on their writing. However, high procrastinators wrote their papers early only when they received feedback." Receiving feedback almost entirely negated procrastinatory tendencies for the specific task under investigation, leading authors to suggest that feedback could complement counselling interventions.

When the deadline being avoided is still distant, procrastinators report significantly less stress than non-procrastinators. Additionally they report fewer symptoms of physical illness. However, as the deadline approaches, this relationship is reversed; procrastinators report more stress, more symptoms of physical illness, and more medical visits. Weighting equally measures at the beginning and

end of the semester, it appears as though the short-term health benefits of procrastination are more than made up for by later health problems.

Procrastinators experience significantly more symptoms of illness and stress than do non-procrastinators as the deadline is upon them, to the extent that, overall, procrastinators had suffered more stress and health problems.

References

Tice, D. M., & Baumeister, R. F. (1997) Longitudinal Study of Procrastination, Performance, Stress, and Health: The Costs and Benefits of Dawdling

Wikipedia

Pychyl, T. A., Lee, J. M., Thibodeau, R., & Blunt, A. (2000). Five days of emotion: An experience sampling study of undergraduate student procrastination (special issue). Journal of Social Behavior and Personality, 15, 239-254.

Fritzsche, B. A., Young, B. R., & Hickson, K. C. (2003) Individual differences in academic procrastination tendency and writing success

Robert B. Slaney is a professor of counseling psychology in Penn State's College of Education

McGarvey. Jason A. (1996) The Almost Perfect Definition

Perfectionism

The All-or-Nothing Mindset

To Escape Criticism — Do Nothing, Say Nothing, Be Nothing

"A man would do nothing if he waited until he could do it so well that no one could find fault", John Henry Newman says. This is known as perfectionism.

Perfectionism, in psychology, is a personality trait characterized by a person's striving for flawlessness and setting excessively high performance standards, accompanied by overly critical self-evaluations and concerns regarding others' evaluations.

It is best conceptualized as a multidimensional characteristic, as psychologists agree that there are many positive and negative aspects. In its maladaptive form, perfectionism drives people to attempt to achieve an unattainable ideal, and their adaptive perfectionism can sometimes motivate them to reach their goals. In the end, they derive pleasure from doing so. When perfectionists do not reach their goals, they often fall into depression.

Perfectionists strain compulsively and unceasingly toward unobtainable goals, and measure their self-worth by productivity and accomplishment. Pressuring oneself to achieve unrealistic goals inevitably sets the person up for disappointment. Perfectionists tend to be harsh critics of themselves when they fail to meet their standards.

Traditionally, procrastination has been associated with perfectionism, a tendency to negatively evaluate outcomes and one's own performance, intense fear and avoidance of evaluation of one's abilities by others, heightened social self-consciousness and anxiety, recurrent low mood, and "workaholism".

General Applications

Perfectionism often shows up in performance at work or school, neatness and aesthetics, organization, writing, speaking, physical appearance, and health and personal cleanliness.

In the workplace, perfectionism is often marked by low productivity and missed deadlines as people lose time and energy by paying attention to irrelevant details of their tasks, ranging from major projects to mundane daily activities.

This can lead to depression, social alienation, and a greater risk of workplace "accidents." Adderholdt-Elliot (1989) describes five characteristics of perfectionist students and teachers which contribute to underachievement: procrastination, fear of failure, an "all-or-nothing" mindset, paralysed perfectionism, and workaholism.

According to C. Allen, in intimate relationships, unrealistic expectations can cause significant dissatisfaction for both partners. Greenspon lists behaviors, thoughts, and feelings that typically characterize perfectionism.

Perfectionists will not be content with their work until it meets their standards, which can make perfectionists less efficient in finishing projects, and they therefore will struggle to meet deadlines.

Medical Complications

Perfectionists can suffer anxiety and low self-esteem. Perfectionism is a risk factor for obsessive compulsive disorder, obsessive compulsive personality disorder, eating disorders, social anxiety, social phobia, body dysmorphic disorder, workaholism, self harm, substance abuse, and clinical depression as well as physical problems like chronic stress, and heart disease. In addition, studies have found that people with perfectionism have a higher mortality rate than those without perfectionism. A possible reason for this is the additional stress and worry that accompanies the irrational belief that everything should be perfect.

Therapists attempt to tackle the negative thinking that surrounds perfectionism, in particular the "all-or-nothing" thinking in which the client believes that an achievement is either perfect or useless. They encourage clients to set realistic goals and to face their fear of failure.

Since perfectionism is a self-esteem issue based on emotional convictions about what one must do to be acceptable as a person, negative thinking is most successfully addressed in the context of a recovery process which directly addresses these emotional convictions.

Normal Vs. Neurotic Perfectionists

Hamachek was one of the first psychologists to argue for two distinct types of perfectionism, classifying people as normal perfectionists or neurotic perfectionists. Normal perfectionists pursue perfection without compromising their self-esteem, and derive pleasure from their efforts. Neurotic perfectionists strive for unrealistic goals and consistently feel dissatisfied when they cannot reach them.

"Well, dear, we finally finished reading all the manuals to life. Shall we go out and do some living now?"

Researchers have begun to investigate the role of perfectionism in various mental disorders such as depression, anxiety, eating disorders and personality disorders. Each disorder has varying levels of the three measures on the MPS-scale (Multidimensional

Perfectionism Scale). Socially prescribed perfectionism in young women has been associated with greater body-image dissatisfaction and avoidance of social situations that focus on weight and physical appearance.

Negative aspects

In its pathological form, perfectionism can be damaging. It can take the form of procrastination when used to postpone tasks and self-deprecation when used to excuse poor performance or to seek sympathy and affirmation from other people. In general, maladaptive perfectionists feel constant pressure to meet their high standards, which creates cognitive dissonance when one cannot meet their own expectations. Perfectionism has been associated with numerous other psychological and physiological complications as well.

Hillary Rettig, author of book The 7 Secrets of the Prolific: The Definitive Guide to Overcoming Procrastination, Perfectionism, and Writer's Block, has identified on her blog five major characteristics of perfectionists, including:

Defining success narrowly and unrealistically; punishing oneself harshly for perceived failures – A perfectionist perceives her outcomes as being worse than they really are.

Grandiosity – The deluded idea that things that are difficult for other people should be easy for you.

Shortsightedness – Manifested in a "now or never" or "do or die" attitude.

> *saha-jam karma kaunteya*
> *sa-dosam api na tyajet*
> *sarvarambha hi dosena*
> *dhumenagnir ivavrtah*
>
> *Every endeavor is covered by some fault, just as fire is covered by smoke. Therefore one should not give up the work born of his nature, O son of Kunti, even if such work is full of fault.*
>
> *A very nice example is given herein. Although fire is pure, still there is smoke. Yet smoke does not make the fire impure. Even though there is smoke in the fire, fire is still considered to be the purest of all elements. If one prefers to give up the work of a ksatriya and take up the occupation of a brahmana, he is not assured that in the occupation of a brahmana there are no unpleasant duties. One may then conclude that in the material world no one can be completely free from the contamination of material nature. This example of fire and smoke is very appropriate in this connection. When in wintertime one takes a stone from the fire, sometimes smoke disturbs the eyes and other parts of the body, but still one must make use of the fire despite disturbing conditions. Similarly, one should not give up his natural occupation because there are some disturbing elements. Rather, one should be determined to serve the Supreme Lord by his occupational duty in Krsna consciousness. That is the perfectional point. When a particular type of occupation is performed for the satisfaction of the Supreme Lord, all the defects in that particular occupation are purified. When the results of work are purified, when connected with devotional service, one becomes perfect in seeing the self within, and that is self-realization.*
>
> *~ Srila Prabhupada (Bhagavad-gita 18.48)*

Overidentification with work – When things are going well, a perfectionist feels like king or queen of the world, and if it fails, he or she is down in the dumps.

Overemphasis on product (vs. process), and on external rewards. – Perfectionists are obsessed with how good the final result of their efforts will be, and the reward they hope to reap.

Rettig also lists ten minor characteristics of perfectionism:

Labeling – Harshly branding oneself with terms like stupid, lazy, wimpy, etc.

Hyperbole – Overstating the negative.

Fetishes – A perfectionist fetish can be any relentlessly repetitive form of self-criticism.

Dichotomizing – A perfectionist often sees things in black-and-white terms, with no shades of gray.

Competitiveness / Comparisons – Perfectionist often draw comparisons unfairly using themselves at their peak level of performance.

Unconscious Process – A perfectionist often "wings it" instead of using an informed strategy.

Pathologizing of Normal Work Processes or Events – A perfectionist will not accept that they can have a "bad" or "off" day and instead will use a normal event as evidence of their own failure.

Negativity – A perfectionist habitually undervalues themselves, their accomplishments, others' accomplishments, and also others' willingness to help.

Rigidity – A perfectionist persists in trying the same nonworking solutions over and over.

Blind Spots / Misplaced Pride – A perfectionist often confuses "high standards" with "impossible standards."

References

Stoeber, Joachim; Childs, Julian H. (2010). "The Assessment of Self-Oriented and Socially Prescribed Perfectionism: Subscales Make a Difference". Journal of Personality Assessment 92 (6): 577–585. doi:10.1080/00223891.2010.513306. PMID 20954059.

Flett, G. L.; Hewitt, P. L. (2002). Perfectionism. Washington, DC: American Psychological Association. pp. 5–31.

Yang, Hongfei; Stoeber, Joachim (2012). "The Physical Appearance Perfectionism Scale: Development and Preliminary Validation". Journal of Psychopathology and Behavioral Assessment 34 (1): 69–83. doi:10.1007/s10862-011-9260-7.

Parker, W. D.; Adkins, K. K. (1995). "Perfectionism and the gifted". Roeper Review 17 (3): 173–176. doi:10.1080/02783199509553653.

Hamachek, D. E. (1978). "Psychodynamics of normal and neurotic perfectionism". Psychology 15: 27–33

Rice, Kenneth G.; Ashby, Jeffrey S., Gilman, Rich (2011). "Classifying adolescent perfectionists". Psychological Assessment 23 (3): 563–577. doi:10.1037/a0022482. PMID 21319903.

Stoeber, Joachim; Otto, Kathleen (2006). "Positive Conceptions of Perfectionism: Approaches, Evidence, Challenges". Personality and Social Psychology Review 10 (4): 295–319. doi:10.1207/s15327957pspr1004_2. PMID 17201590.

Frost, R. O.; Heimburg, R. G.; Holt, C. S.; Mattia, J. I.; Neubauer, A. A. (1993). "A comparison of two measures of perfectionism". Personality and Individual Differences 14: 469–489. doi:10.1016/0191-8869(93)90181-2

Greenspon, T.S. (2008). Making sense of error: A view of the origins and treatment of perfectionism. American Journal of Psychotherapy, 62, (3), 263-282.

Greenspon, T.S. (2007)What to do when good enough is not good enough: The real deal on perfectionism. Minneapolis: Free Spirit Publishing.

Academic procrastination

A 1992 study showed that "52% of surveyed students indicated having a moderate to high need for help concerning procrastination". It is estimated that 80%–95% of college students engage in procrastination, approximately 75% considering themselves procrastinators.

One source of procrastination is the planning fallacy, where we underestimate the time required to analyze research. Many students devote weeks to gathering research for a term paper, but are unable to finish writing it because they have left insufficient time for subsequent stages of the assignment.

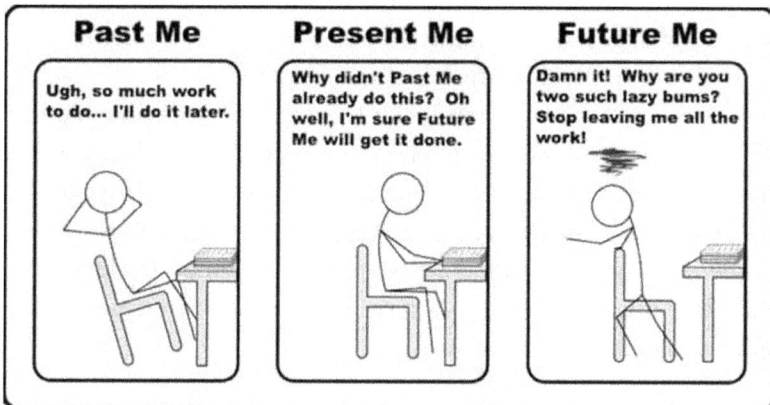

Similarly, students know better than anyone whether or not an assignment or task is feasible. Many students believe in the common method of cramming when studying for an exam or writing up a research paper in one sitting rather than spacing everything out.

Despite the stress, lack of sleep, and inefficiency involved, students become trapped into a perpetual mode of procrastination.

"Student syndrome" refers to the phenomenon where a student will only begin to fully apply themselves to a task immediately before a deadline. This negates the usefulness of any buffers built into individual task duration estimates. Study results indicate that many students are aware of procrastination and accordingly set binding deadlines long before the date for which the task is due.

Furthermore, these self-imposed binding deadlines are correlated with a better performance than without binding deadlines, though performance is best for evenly-spaced external binding deadlines.

In one experiment, participation in online exercises was found to be five times higher in the final week before a deadline than in the summed total of the first three weeks for which the exercises were available. Procrastinators end up being the ones doing most of the work in the final week before a deadline.

Other reasons cited on why students procrastinate include fear of failure and success, perfectionist expectations, and legitimate activities that may take precedence over school work (like a job).

Procrastination has been associated with the later submission of academic papers, as would have been expected almost by definition. Additionally, procrastinators have been found to receive worse grades that do non-procrastinators.

Tice et al. (1997) report that more than one third of variation in final exam score could be attributed to procrastination. The negative association between procrastination and academic performance is recurring and consistent.

Different findings emerge when observed and self-report procrastination are contrasted.

There is a point in every student's life that they can't seem to focus on one thing. Whether it's going to work out, starting a diet, and of course, finishing that 10 page essay. Students know their priorities but instead will put it to the last minute. In some studies, people believe that students tend to have an adrenaline rush and think they will do better if they work under pressure.

References

http://calnewport.com/blog/2011/07/10/the-procrastinating-caveman-what-human-evolution-teaches-us-about-why-we-put-off-work-and-how-to-stop/

Wikipedia

Ariely, Dan; Wertenbroch, Klaus (2002). "Procrastination, Deadlines, and Performance: Self-Control by Precommitment". Psychological Science 13 (3): 219–224. doi:10.1111/1467-9280.00441. PMID 12009041.

"Procrastination — The Writing Center at UNC-Chapel Hill". Writingcenter.unc.edu.

Tuckman, B. W., (1991) The Development and Concurrent Validity of the Procrastination Scale

THE AUTHOR

Dr. Sahadeva dasa (Sanjay Shah) is a monk in vaisnava tradition. His areas of work include research in Vedic and contemporary thought, Corporate and educational training, social work and counselling, travelling, writing books and of course, practicing spiritual life and spreading awareness about the same.

He is also an accomplished musician, composer, singer, instruments player and sound engineer. He has more than a dozen albums to his credit so far. (SoulMelodies.com)

His varied interests include alternative holistic living, Vedic studies, social criticism, environment, linguistics, history, art & crafts, nature studies, web technologies etc.

Many of his books have been acclaimed internationally and translated in other languages.

By The Same Author

Oil-Final Countdown To A Global Crisis And Its Solutions

End of Modern Civilization And Alternative Future

To Kill Cow Means To End Human Civilization

Cow And Humanity - Made For Each Other

Cows Are Cool - Love 'Em!

Let's Be Friends - A Curious, Calm Cow

Wondrous Glories of Vraja

We Feel Just Like You Do

Tsunami Of Diseases Headed Our Way - Know Your Food Before Time Runs Out

Cow Killing And Beef Export - The Master Plan To Turn India Into A Desert

By 2050

Capitalism Communism And Cowism - A New Economics For The 21st Century

Noble Cow - Munching Grass, Looking Curious And Just Hanging Around

World - Through The Eyes Of Scriptures

To Save Time Is To Lengthen Life

Life Is Nothing But Time - Time Is Life, Life Is Time

Lost Time Is Never Found Again

Spare Us Some Carcasses - An Appeal From The Vultures

Cow Dung - A Down-To- Earth Solution To Global Warming And Climate

Change

Cow Dung For Food Security And Survival of Human Race

(More information on availability on DrDasa.com)

www.ingramcontent.com/pod-product-compliance
Lightning Source LLC
Chambersburg PA
CBHW070640030426
42337CB00020B/4096